Dialogues

English Studies in India

Dialogues
English Studies in India

Edited by
Rachna Sethi
A.L. Khanna

AAKAR

Dialogues: English Studies in India
Edited by Rachna Sethi and A.L. Khanna

First Published 2020

ISBN 978-93-5002-626-7

Published by
AAKAR BOOKS
28 E Pocket IV, Mayur Vihar Phase I
Delhi 110 091 India
aakarbooks@gmail.com

Laser Typeset at
Arpit Printographers, Delhi

Printed at
D.K. Fine Art Press, Delhi

Forum for Teachers of English Language and Literature (FORTELL)

FORTELL (Forum for Teachers of English Language and Literature), an autonomous body, set up in 1989 by about one hundred English school and college teachers in Delhi, has grown into an all India English teachers' organization in the last three decades. It is an affiliate of TESOL (Teachers of English to Speakers of Other Languages), USA and IATEFL (International Association of Teachers of English as a Foreign Language), UK. It has organized several workshops and seminars over the years in areas like curriculum design, materials development and pedagogical practices.

FORTELL: **Journal of Teaching English Language and Literature** is a bi-annual, peer-reviewed journal available in both print (ISSN 2229-6557) and online versions (ISSN 2394-9244). The entire archive through its open access policy is available on the website (www.fortell.org). *FORTELL* provides a forum for exchange of ideas related to theory, principles and practices that govern teaching of English language and literature in India and elsewhere in the world. By addressing wide-ranging concerns of researchers and practitioners from the field, it plays a significant role as an interface between school teaching and higher education.

Foreign Languages University, Hyderabad, Telengana

Anju Sahgal Gupta, Professor, School of Humanities, Indira Gandhi National Open University, New Delhi

Raj Kumar, Professor and Head, Department of English, University of Delhi, Delhi

Simi Malhotra, Professor, Department of English & Director, Centre for North East Studies and Policy Research, Jamia Millia Islamia, New Delhi

G.J.V. Prasad, Professor, Centre for English Studies, School of Language, Literature and Cultural Studies, Jawaharlal Nehru University, New Delhi

Ronald Strickland, Professor and Department Chair, Humanities, Michigan Technological University, USA

Jacob Tharu, Formerly Professor, Department of Testing and Evaluation, English and Foreign Languages University, Hyderabad, Telengana

Brian Tomlinson, Visiting Professor, Azad University, Oxford and Leeds Metropolitan University, UK

Contents

Future Directions

Introduction

This book brings together a collection of interviews under the broad rubric of English Studies in India, and deals with a diverse range of topics from translation to interdisciplinarity to academic writing. Not only are the themes under discussion wide-ranging but the interviewees cover the global breadth, including English academics from different parts of India and the world. These interviews were originally published in *FORTELL* journal over the last decade and a half. The journal is the most visible and recognizable face of FORTELL (Forum for Teachers of English Language and Literature), an autonomous body of English teaching professionals founded in 1989. The bi-annual peer-reviewed journal apart from articles, publishes an 'Interview' in every issue that raises important concerns about curricula, pedagogy and changing paradigms of English education in India.

By bringing forth conversations where both the interviewee and the interviewer are academics, the anthology places before the readers multifarious voices. From the in-between space of loud-thinking and reflection; of public and personal interaction; of rambling and well-formulated arguments, a polyphony of voices and views about English Studies comes across in these dialogues. As opposed to the rigid structure of an article, the thoughts in an interview are expressed in a fluid space that the interviewer and interviewee negotiate, and the reader is invited to enter this interactive thought-process. This volume gives primacy to the form of the dialogue/interview and wants the multiple perspectives and subjectivities to 'speak' directly to the reader, and consciously refrains from giving a 'guided tour' of the English discipline. The latter is also a difficult task as the dialogues are polysemic voices reflecting on the two-way causality of theoretical paradigms and curricula, and both are 'tested' in the dynamic platform of the classroom.

Dialogues

The discussions in the interviews interrogate policy and practice pertaining to English Studies, and the dialogues between academics bring forth the pertinent concerns of teaching English in India. Dialogue is historically and philosophically an important way of unravelling and debating ideas. Socratic dialogue is a literary genre whereby a group of people guided by a facilitator try to explore complex ideas 'to get to the truth of things, to open up issues and problems, to uncover assumptions, to analyze concepts, to distinguish what is known from what is not known' (Paul and Elder, 2007, p. 36). The systematic and disciplined questioning focuses on foundational concepts, principles, theories and issues; these are considered by the group in a cooperative search for a 'universal truth', through citing personal examples and experiences. Dualism or the dialectic, rather than singularity of views lies at the heart of dialogue.

While the conversations here do not exactly follow the 'Socratic method', but discussions and concerns about English language and literature lie at the heart of it. Through dialogue, the 'interview' becomes a joint reflection on a theme, as issues are elaborated and debated, unravelling for the reader a greater understanding about the discipline. The insights are developed in this case through conversation, a two-way process of exchange, rather than a one-way treatise. Since the 'interviewer' is not a lay person but a co-academic/researcher, the dialogue held in 'private' brings forth important debates in 'public' space through publication. Maurice Friedman (1983) writes that it is the 'between' (*entre*) that reveals, that permits understanding. It is not through the *I* or *you*, but rather through the *our*, the between that discovery takes place.

It is in the overlapping and shared space of the *between*, that understanding develops about the issues being discussed.

Heidegger has asserted (1969) that 'the very act of posing a question is disclosure, for a question is to sketch in advance the context of meaning in which a particular inquiry will move (p. 269).' The answering in turn can lead to counter-questioning or revision of view of the interviewer, thus the dialogue is shaped by both. Dialogue is in the realm of the oral, and can be rambling and tentative, as opposed to the more coherent and cogently put written arguments. However the 'thinking aloud' or oral also offers an unguarded revealing, an intimate outpouring offering a direct experiential access, and revealing complexity of thoughts in the process. While some interviews were conducted over email, most were held face to face, recorded in person, and the exchanges were subsequently transcribed. While 'verbatim' tries its best to capture the spontaneity, one is aware that the written/typed word loses in 'recording' the non-verbal communication, the body language, the twinkling of the eye, the tone or laughter. We hope that despite the limitations of the written/typed word, the dialogues and discussions will lead to greater engagement about the concerned issues.

English Studies in India

The interviews can be read as mapping, interrogating and suggesting future directions for English Studies in India. English was introduced in India during the colonial rule, and learners were introduced to a literary canon comprising of Chaucer, Shakespeare, Milton, Dryden, Wordsworth and the likes that were presented as the finest in literature. Independence in 1947 placed before the leaders the task of finding a national language, and none of the Indian languages could claim superiority to the others. With no consensus in place, the debate narrowed on two languages- Hindi and English. Hindi faced strong resistance from the South, and in 1950 the Constitution of India stipulated that Hindi in the

Devnagri script would be the official language of the Union of India and laid down a time frame of 15 years to effect the change over from English to Hindi. However that never happened and in 1967, the Official Languages (Amendment) Act made English an associate language of the Union of India without any time limit.

While the debates regarding English, including among other things, education policy about the language of instruction continued, from the 1980s onwards a questioning of the literary canon gained momentum. Gauri Viswanathan in *Masks of Conquests: Literary Study and British Rule in India* (1989) observes that the English canon was offered to the Indian student with a view to present a formidable image of the ruling class: 'the English literary text, functioning as a surrogate Englishman in his highest and most perfect state, becomes a mask for economic exploitation ... successfully camouflaging the material activities of the colonizer' (p. 20). In the 1980s and 1990s, Indian academia witnessed an interrogation of colonial concerns in English literary studies, and a series of seminars and conferences deliberated upon the crisis. Works like *The Lie of the Land: English Literary Studies in India* (ed. Rajeswari Sunder Rajan, 1992); *Provocations: The Teaching of English Literature in India* (ed. Sudhakar Marathe et al., 1993); *Rethinking English: Essays in Literature, Language, History* (ed. Svati Joshi, 1994); and *Subject to Change: Teaching Literature in the Nineties* (ed. Susie Tharu, 1998) questioned the disciplinary formation of English in India and the politics of literary studies.

The re-readings of the canon underlined the politics of exclusion implicit in the creation of literary canons. The theoretical deliberations on decanonization led to syllabi revisions of English Studies, and brought a shift from 'English literature' to 'Literatures in English'; however the process has been varied and non-uniform across universities. The decanonization branched out to include the following: literatures in other Englishes (Indian, American, African,

Caribbean etc.); world literature (in English translation); introduction of Indian classical aesthetics; and Indian literature (read primarily in English). Reading texts from different Indian (and foreign) languages in English departments necessitates a rethinking about translation and raises questions like: Do English translations (re)establish the dominance of English or decentre it? How are power dynamics of languages negotiated through translation? Does the coexistence of languages make space for multilingualism in the classroom?

The Centre for English Studies, JNU was amongst the first to herald changes in English curricula in the 1980s, and the syllabus revision of the University of Delhi in 1999 was celebrated as 'revolutionary'. The shift from English literature to world literatures, with focus on Indian Writing in English and Indian Writing in (English) translation, was the trend followed by other universities, with the process being spread over decades in the country. Apart from the wider expanse of literature in curricula, the CBCS syllabus has included papers like 'Academic Writing' and 'Creative Writing' to focus on development of skills. Ravindra B. Tasildar in *English Studies in India: The Present Scenario* (2018) evaluates the contemporary situation of the discipline in the country by reviewing the syllabi of BA, MA, MPhil courses offered in about 50 Indian universities in the first decade of the twenty-first century. Along with focusing on established trends, he points towards the possible changes needed in the future.

With more than two decades since the 'alternative canon' (which has now become the norm) was adopted, it is time to question its premises, and search for new directions in the globalized era. A three-day conference on 'Interrogating English Studies in India' organized by Bharati College, University of Delhi, held in association with FORTELL, and supported by ICSSR and Sahitya Akademi in February 2014 was an attempt in this direction. It highlighted the urgency of rethinking the objectives of English Studies in India, given the contemporary scenario of technological advancement and the changing needs of the student in the class (Anavisha Banerjee). Ania Loomba in her keynote address focused on the difference between English Studies and English literature studies. Rukmini Bhaya Nair's paper, 'Talking back to Technology' emphasized the role of technology in the construction of language.

Today English Studies in India needs to be reoriented to suit the requirements of the globalized world. Reformulation is needed in three major areas in English departments to deal with the dynamic changes around us. First, the discipline needs to be redefined to make space and is creating space for other media, like visual media, film studies, cyber literature and blogs. Second, one needs to harness the vast potential of technology in the classroom, and acknowledge the advantages of blended learning. Third, to rethink the role of language teaching in English departments. The last point has been repeatedly discussed by academics in the course of the interviews; and while there is no consensus on whether we need literature to teach language, there is agreement that vast majority of people aspire to learn English for getting jobs and for social mobility. The globalized world has made it imperative that there be a shift in axis to include modules like Communication English and English for Special Purposes (ESP) as language is an economic commodity in the market. Employability cannot be divorced from learning of English in view of glocal needs of the students.

Commenting on changes in English language teaching, Agnihotri, Gupta and Khanna (2017) write that the three most distinguishing features of the contemporary trends in language teaching are 'learner-centredness, reorientation of teacher education and recognition of linguistic and cultural diversity seen in any classroom.'(p. 2) ICT has stormed its way into ELT and Kim discusses how the web tools in the classroom provide an integrated environment for teachers and students. Technologies used may be synchronous (done in real time), such as Skype, Moodle or virtual live classes; or they may be asynchronous (not done in real time) such as podcasts and blogs.' (Eaton, 2010, p. 14). MALL (Mobile Assisted Language Learning) is quickly gaining as much buzz today as CALL (Computer Assisted Language Learning) created in the 1980s and 1990s.

Tasildar (2018) emphasizes that the biggest need is to shift focus from 'an imaginary ideal learner' to know 'how learners, the real stakeholders, perceive their own academic predicament.' (p. 14) While technology and the needs-driven world is pushing for student-centric classrooms, the teacher needs to not just update knowledge but tech-knowledge, and also have socially conscious pedagogy that incorporates disability and caste into the classroom. Instead of discussing replacement of the teacher by apps, we need to focus on teacher training to prepare them for the changes sweeping in, and more of that is discussed in the next section.

Themes and Concerns

The book has been divided into four sections: (Re)defining English Studies; Pedagogical Challenges; Professional Development of Teachers; and Future Directions.

The first section, '(Re)defining English Studies' deliberates upon the changing mandate for English departments in India. Over the last couple of decades, the curriculum and research of English departments reflect certain common trends like inclusion of literatures from around the world, Indian literatures in translation, folk traditions and Cultural Studies. The interviewees discuss both the excitement and the flip side of co-opting of Indian languages and literature in English Studies.

Harish Trivedi reflects upon his mixed feelings regarding the 'revolutionary syllabus' change that happened in the University of Delhi during his tenure as Head, Department of English. He feels that while it gave students greater exposure to literatures in other Indian languages through translated texts, it also gives them the mistaken notion that they know quite a lot about Indian literature. He feels that people who need functional English language skills do not have to be taught Shakespeare, 'language need not be taught through literary and hoary literary classics'. He suggests having a separate department for English Language Teaching where functional English is taught as most people in India want a mid-level skill through learning the language.

Makarand R. Paranjape discusses the multidirectional causality between economic power and literary/cultural power. He feels that while the creative resources of English have been exploited, what is expected is a greater expansion in market of other languages to provide a counter balance to dominance of English. As for the dilemma of how to teach/whether to teach literature and/or language, he suggests a model where practical courses like Business English and Communication English are taught to people to land jobs and 'literature should be left for fewer people who are deeply interested in it'.

G.J.V. Prasad reflects on the possible directions that English departments in India could have taken: either to specialize in language teaching or to focus on literary studies. He feels that English departments are reinventing themselves into Cultural Studies departments, and this has made possible the co-opting of Indian languages, and one can research on Hindi or Tamil literature in the English departments. He discusses the contemporary interdisciplinary thrust in Higher Education and how it makes new research exciting, but he cautions that 'humility and admittance of lack of knowledge about other disciplines has been replaced by brashness'. He feels that the teacher/guide is equipped with 'a tool kit' of different disciplines and it his/her responsibility to train the students in functions of the tools and their origins, so that the students can use the appropriate one for decoding the text.

Christel R. Devadawson discusses the need to think of literature beyond its textual definition, and suggests engaging with genre fluidity in classrooms. She reiterates that despite the changes sweeping across Higher Education vis-à-vis the fluid space of the discipline and syllabi revisions, the 'keystone in the academic arch will be and always has been the student in the classroom'.

The second section, 'Pedagogical Challenges' raises concerns from academics about the dynamics of the classroom and the changing roles of the teacher. The interviewees repeatedly echo the need to reinvent pedagogy from the traditional teacher-centric approach. The Indian education system often treats the students as passive recipients, but for an effective teaching-learning process the student has to be recognized as the keystone and has to be a participant in the making of meaning. The section suggests that perhaps teachers need to reassess their approaches which are based in their comfort zones and instead focus on the process rather than the product/answer.

Rama Kant Agnihotri while discussing the nature of language, emphasizes that while for people in power, the concept of 'a language' is sacred and is treated as homogeneous; the language of the common people and of the material world is fluid where languages flow into each other, 'words travel, they do not need passports like humans'. He feels that human language capacity should be defined as multilinguality and fluidity for him constitutes the core of multilinguality; historically, that's the way all languages came into being, and that is how languages travel. To capitalize on multilingualism in the classroom as a resource, it should be emphasized in teacher training whereby teachers are made conscious that all languages, irrespective of whether they are called dialect, *dehati* or *khichri* are equally rich.

Rimli Bhattacharya elaborates on a wide range of issues related to children's literature: problematics of definition, 'appropriate' themes, market pressures and value education. She observes that 'contemporary globalization turns everything from poetry or pizza into a product'. She discusses in detail the 'creation' of textbooks which are often accompanied by an impossible wish list whereby everything that we are not, we want the children to be. This overriding concern defines the choice of lessons in the textbook, whereby everything tries to reflect the ideal. She cautions against viewing textbooks as 'finished' products, with fixed texts and exercises; instead she sees 'the texts in a textbook in a provisional form, with which the process of learning and teaching begins'. She emphasizes that thought, planning and teacher training all go into a dynamic classroom interaction where a text can 'come alive for and through the child'.

Jonathan Gil Harris shares his experience of teaching in Indian universities which made him realize that he needed to devise different kinds of writing assignments to engage the students more effectively. He encouraged his students to deal with texts creatively, and move beyond idolatory, even if it is Shakespeare, and think besides arriving at the 'right' meaning. He emphasizes that learning cannot happen when students are passive recipients, for it to be effective 'the student has to become a marker of meaning too'. Harris discusses his mixed views about aligning literature and language teaching. On one hand he feels that 'to teach literature is to teach language' as literature is artful use of language. On the other hand, he does not believe that 'literature and language teaching should be collapsed into each other' as teaching Shakespeare's dramatic verse is quite different from teaching academic writing to engineering students.

Jackie-Lynn Van Tilburgh shares her experience of the Indian classroom as part of the English Language Fellow Program. She observes that students prefer being tested on reading and writing skills over speaking skills as the latter makes them self-conscious and exposes their mistakes publicly. Even with writing, the focus is not on the process of writing in the Indian scenario; and she discusses the academic writing courses that she ran where students were taught to make outlines, revise drafts, and at the end of the course they could appreciate the difference it made to their work, rather than writing the assignment the day before it is due.

Dee Broughton too points out that the Indian education system is not geared towards training students in writing. She reiterates that there is need for a paradigm shift in approach, where the goal should not be 'to produce a perfect paragraph about a particular poem or story' but to 'produce a student body that is capable of writing a paragraph about anything'. She feels that teachers should be trained to introduce academic writing at undergraduate level itself. Penny Ur's views move beyond the Indian context; she discusses English as a lingua franca (EFL). She feels that ELF will be a 'standard' variety of English to be universally comprehensible but will in all probability embrace a range of forms and usages.

The third section, 'Professional Development of Teachers' is linked to the previous section as professional development helps create the dynamic classroom atmosphere. To keep himself/herself abreast of recent researches and practices of teaching, and to invigorate pedagogy, CPD (Continuous Professional Development) is essential for teachers.

N.S. Prabhu believes that teachers' growth arises from the process of thinking about and making sense of their classroom experiences. He argues for an active, engaging role by teachers for their professional development that can be supported by others (trainers, specialists). Rod Bolitho stresses upon observation and supervision, as part of the development process, and reiterates that the product should not be privileged over the process. He details four dilemmas that a practitioner must negotiate to derive value: to understand we all have 'Baggage' of our views; 'Perception Gap', i.e. different perspectives people have of the same event; 'Impact of the Observer's Presence in the Classroom'; and 'Feedback'.

Rama Mathew shares her views on assessment, and categorizes it into SA (summative assessment) and FA (formative assessment). SA is sum-total of learning in a year, the 'product' of learning while FA is a commitment to understand learning during the 'process' of learning. While SA is externally designed and managed, FA is the teacher's responsibility; Mathew insists that assessment is all about practice and it is crucial that teachers be trained in it. Shobha Sinha opines that the impact of poor teaching is immediately visible in the faces of the students, and underlines that there is no choice but to have professional development for teachers. She emphasizes that enabling context is essential for CPD and development can take place only through dialogue.

The fourth section, 'Future Directions' takes us back to the first section which had redefined and expanded the definition of English Studies in India. It makes one question if the decanoization has created an alternative canon that is now the 'trend'. It also suggests possible areas that need to be included into mainstream teaching, like Dalit Studies and Disability Studies. The technology-driven world is today not just defining 'What we teach' but 'How we teach'; and e-learning and mobile learning are no longer fancy tags but technologies that the teacher today needs to keep abreast of. Blended learning is repeatedly posited as the future that combines the best elements of online and classroom learning.

Saugata Bhaduri discusses the decanonization process that the Centre for English Studies, JNU initiated in English Studies in the mid-1980s and he feels that about three decades later, the 'radical' syllabi has become the norm that every English department in India has subsequently followed. He suggests some of the ways for further decanonization include focusing on domains like Dalit Studies, Disability Studies, Ecocriticism and to include cyberculture and new media as objects of 'literary' study. He argues for a 'disruptive, subversive inclusion of the profane and the popular in the classroom'. He emphasizes that popular culture and media studies comprise the very ontology of literary studies in post-print mediatized environment.

Raj Kumar points out that caste prejudices are still prevalent in academia, while radicalism is visible in public space, rigidity and customs continue to dominate in personal space. He feels that it is essential to bring caste into the discursive space of the classroom, and one of the ways is by offering courses on Dalit Literature. He stresses that it is important to raise caste issues through pedagogy as students can be future agents of change. Hemachandran Karah discusses the issue of inclusive education regarding disability, and points out that apart from making audio and braille books available, one has to acknowledge that 'in an unequal marathon like ours, students start at different points'. He feels that disability pedagogy should be an integral component in teacher-training for teachers to understand the needs of special students in the classroom.

Pushpinder Syal addresses the shifts in the discipline with reference to the pervasive presence of technology. She stresses that in a tech-enabled classroom, the role of the teacher is that of the facilitator, and he/she needs to be well-versed in the use of web-tools, and should be able to guide the students 'to critically monitor the ideology that underlies the programmes'. Pete Sharma delves into details of blended learning and suggests that its effectiveness lies in harnessing the best elements of both classroom and online learning. In an era of TELL (technology enhanced learning), teaching is about creating optimum conditions for learning where the role of the teacher has shifted from being 'sage on the stage' to 'guide on the side'. He feels that since apps encourage autonomous learning, the teachers need to reinvent themselves, and 'technology is less unlikely to replace the creative teacher'.

The dialogue with Richard Allen shifts the focus from the Indian classrooms to the larger global concern of blended learning in the context of off-campus learning. He discusses the three keys for development of distance learning: quality leaning, student interactivity, and technology enabled interactivity. With reference to English Studies, Allen gives technology-assisted examples that are carried out at Open University, UK like hyperlinked edition of texts; computer-based assistants for language learning; and online conferences for creative writing workshops.

The conversations in this volume deal with a wide spectrum of issues concerning English studies in India. *Dialogues* does not posit solutions to complex situations and problems that English teachers face, instead it opens the field for deliberations. The conversations here present varied points of view, and hope to encourage engagement with these themes through research and classroom practices.

References

Agnihotri, R.K., Gupta, A.S. and Khanna, A.L. (eds.) (2017). *Trends in Language Teaching*. New Delhi: Orient BlackSwan.

Banerjee, A. (2014). 'Report: Interrogating English Studies in India.' *Fortell*, Issue No. 29. http://www.fortell.org/content/interrogating-english-studies-india

Eaton, S.E. (2010). *Global Trends in Language Teaching in the 21st Century*. Calgary: Onate Press.

Friedman, M. (1983). *The Confirmation of Otherness in Family, Community, and Society*. New York: Pilgrim.

Heidegger, M. (1969). In W.H. Bossart, 'Three Directions of Phenomenology' in M. Greene (ed.), *The Anatomy of Knowledge*. Amherst: University of Massachussets Press.

Joshi, S. (ed.) (1991). *Rethinking English: Essays in Literature, Language, History*. New Delhi: Oxford University Press.

Kim,Y. (2011). 'Current Trends in ELT'. *JET*, 1/1, February, 1-13.

Marathe, S., Ramanan, M. and Bellarmine, R. (eds.) *Provocations: The Teaching of English Literature in India*. Madras: Orient Blackswan.

Paul, R. and Elder, L. (2007). 'Critical Thinking: The Art of Socratic Questioning'. *Journal of Developmental Education*, Vol. 31, No. 1, 36-41. https://www.jstor.org/stable/42775632

Rajan, R.S. (ed.) (1992). *The Lie of the Land: English Literary Studies in India*. Delhi: Oxford University Press.

Tasildar, R.B. (2018). *English Studies in India: The Present Scenario*. Newcastle: Cambridge Scholars Publishing.

Tharu, S. (ed.) (1998). *Subject to Change: Teaching Literature in the Nineties*. Delhi: Orient Longman.

Viswanathan, G. (1989). *Masks of Conquest: Literary Study and British Rule in India*. New York: Columbia University Press.

(Re)defining English Studies

1

English is Not Just a Language in India, It is a Dream That We Sell

Harish Trivedi

Interviewed by Mona Sinha and Tasneem Shahnaaz

Mona Sinha and Tasneem Shahnaaz: Sir, you have had a long association with the Department of English, University of Delhi as Professor and Head and you are known for your strong views on the teaching of English and native languages in India. It was during your tenure as Head that a revolutionary syllabus, incorporating large doses of Indian literatures in translation, was introduced for undergraduate students of English literature. We would like to know your views on the current status of English in India and how it is taught in our classrooms.

Harish Trivedi: I'm pleased that we are talking about these issues in a forum which is very well known in the field and which circulates as widely as it does.

About the status of English and as to how it is taught in the classroom, yes, you are right, I have thought about it for a very long time. I feel concerned about it and sometimes I am even anguished about it. If I were asked to name half a dozen major problems in this country, or even maybe just two or three, I would say this is one of them. English is not just a

---

Earlier published in *FORTELL* Issue No. 32 (January 2016), some passages have been restored from the original transcript.

language in India; it is a dream that we sell to any number of people in this country. 'If you learn English, you will get all this, if you don't you will not get any of this. The haves and have-nots will be divided strictly on the basis of whether they know English or not.' —This is what we project so as to bluff the people.

Shahnaaz: Why do you call it a dream or a bluff?

Trivedi: After so many years of teaching English in India, how many people actually know the kind of English that will take them places? Very, very few. Everybody who goes to school begins to learn English in India but 80 to 90 per cent of the people fall by the wayside, unless they have advantages already of the social and economic kind.

There are two or three kinds of English that people acquire in India. One is this top class English that gets you places, that gets you jobs, that makes you succeed in interviews and so on. The second kind of English is fairly correct, competent English but without the accent, without the social bearing to go with it. And that doesn't get you to the top of the tree. And then there is another kind of English which you've learnt for 10 or 12 years in a Hindi-medium school but you are still not much more competent in it than when you started. You might have even got degrees in it. And as I said, this proportion is 80 to 90 per cent of English learners. There are differing statistics about how many people in India know English. Of course, the first thing to do is to define what 'know' is. I would say that figure is not above 5 per cent in any meaningful sense.

But what I'm anguished about is the fact that so many poor people all over India, who can barely earn subsistence-level wages, make great sacrifices to send their children to 'English-medium' schools chasing this impossible dream!

There are two kinds of successes even now possible in India. There are many people who did not know much English but have acquired a smattering along the way as they succeeded. This is the kind represented, for example, by Dhirubhai Ambani. He hardly knew any English when he started, and then his children went to top management schools in the US. The other kind of success is not only Modi; remember also Kamraj, Deve Gowda and Chandra Shekhar, who became top political leaders. The best thing I have heard on this is: *Paanch saal raaj karte hain angrezi mein, aur phir aake vote maangte hain Hindi mein!* (They rule over us for five years in English, and then they come and beg for votes in Hindi!) 'Hindi' here means all our regional languages. So there is a huge paradox at the heart of our democratic nation.

From time to time there are slogans raised, if not movements launched, to remove English from India. I've been watching it with active interest for the last 50 years. It came to a head when Elizabeth II, Queen of England, visited India in 1961. Some of our top socialists and other anti-Congress leaders launched a campaign for removing English from India as a token of assertion and affirmation that we are no longer ruled by the British. One of them was Ram Manohar Lohia who was very attractive to me as a political leader, and quite as charismatic for the young as Nehru.

Here I'd like to mention a couple of short stories in Hindi which bring up the issue of Hindi and English, with English shown as being connected with slavery and snobbery, with people pretending to know English when they don't because otherwise they would be considered to be scum. I sought out two such stories and translated them for an anthology published in London in the year 2000. One of them is titled 'George Pancham ki Naak' ('The Nose of King George V') by Kamleshwar which centres on Queen Elizaberth's visit to India and is as strong a political satire as any. And the other one is by Sharad Joshi, called 'Virginia Woolf se Sab Darte Hain' ('Who's Not Afraid of Virginia Woolf?'), that title being fairly self-explanatory in the Indian context.

So, this is the social situation outside the classroom: a dream of economic and social advancement, as if language alone could do it. I keep arguing against it, but I am also one of the beneficiaries, so I'm a bit compromised!

Let me offer another related argument here. The world's twenty biggest economies are grouped as G-20. Of these, only four or five are English-speaking, because English is their first language. All the other countries have got rich in their own languages, from China to France, from Japan to Germany. We believe that only English will get us there, and this has set India back. So there is a serious national problem here.

Sinha: Can you really wish English away? How do you suggest we get over this hegemonic hold of English over our society?

Trivedi: You're right, and we've perhaps missed the historical opportunities we had. In 1950 it was said we would continue with English only for 15 years. It was not going to continue in perpetuity. But it has now become a vested interest.

Also, we could have had a national language. That would have given us the same situation as Germany and Japan, the same way to grow. But as 1965 approached, the anti-Hindi campaign began in Tamil Nadu and some other states too. They did not want Hindi to be imposed in 1965 and said they wanted more time. Nehru was very concerned about this and assured them that nothing would be imposed upon them against their wishes.

In 2003, I wrote an article in which I said that in our part of the world we can apparently have either a national language or a nation; we can't have both. I mean, just look at Bangladesh breaking away from Pakistan and the Sinhala-Tamil Civil War caused by language as much as by ethnicity in Sri Lanka. And I'm very pleased that in India we still have a nation.

So it is a very difficult situation and there is no easy remedy for this. What can be done is to try and see whether English is equally necessary for everyone in the same proportion. There never will be corporate board-room jobs, English-speaking jobs, for everybody in the country. Many people will have to earn their livelihood in other ways, in their own languages.

Why do they need to learn English and have it thrust down their throats in the same way as others? I am not saying that we should segregate them from the beginning. There should always be opportunities and also the option to switch streams and move forward. Together with English, Hindi has also spread because it has become the language of migration of lower-class labour within the country, of economic mobility and advancement at another level.

Sinha: It is now also the language of the mass media.

Trivedi: When the 24-hour news channels started, it was found that *Aaj Tak* had the highest revenue. Earlier everybody looked down upon Hindi. Now they recognize that Hindi is a force in itself. It's capitalism at work; profits driven not by the elite and the affluent but by a large consumer base.

Sinha: Yes, the top TRP garnering TV channels in the country are in Hindi. English is nowhere close!

Trivedi: And another interesting fact: *The Times of India* calls itself the highest selling English daily in the world. They may be right. But they never tell you that they are *not* the largest selling newspaper in India. The ABC (Audit Bureau of Circulation) tells you that of the 10 largest selling newspapers in India, seven are in Hindi–*Dainik Bhaskar, Dainik Jagran, Panjab Kesri, Amar Ujala* and so on. The basic point here is that there is a hidden strength of the local languages which those of us who operate in English never see.

You asked if there is a way around this. I think it is a bit too late, especially after globalization. But what can be done by us who have English is to recognize that there is another India out there which doesn't. Only when we accord other languages space and dignity will we move towards a true democratization of languages and peoples in India. In Malayalam or Kannada, Tamil or Bangla, the sense of pride in one's own language is so much greater when each of these languages is spoken by 7 or 8 per cent of the population or even less. Hindi is spoken by more than 40 per cent as their first language. And if you add up the number of people who understand Hindi in some form or the other, it brings the figure up to about 70 per cent. That's very large. You can't get by beyond the big cities by just speaking English; you need to know some kind of functional Hindi or other local language.

So let's recognize this situation and let us allocate resources proportionately in the areas of education and development.

Sinha: I wanted to ask you about this other view that English is an Indian language. Very recently, Uday Prakash said this very categorically in an interview to *The Times of India*. Would you agree with this?

Trivedi: For a very long time I did not think so, but now I am changing my mind. Because of Chetan Bhagat and Amish Tripathi! Just look at their sales figures running into millions. If English was not an Indian language would they have been selling so many copies just in India with virtually no international market? Of the 22 Indian languages recognized by the Constitution and the 24 by the Sahitya Akademi, English is no longer at the lowest spot in circulation. A new class of readers has emerged. Earlier English was a badge of elitism. It is now democratic in the sense that large numbers are buying these books. In which other languages does any book sell so many copies? This also means that English has a footprint on the ground in India, especially among our affluent middle class, which we need to recognize.

We need not debate whether English is an Indian language in some deep cultural or emotional sense. I am simply going by the market for novels, and that is a new phenomenon. R.K. Narayan never had it; Raja Rao, Salman Rushdie, Vikram Seth, Arundhati Roy didn't have it. Despite their winning the Booker or other such awards, their sales in India were invisible compared with these sales.

I wrote an article on that recently, published in *Muse India* (Issue No. 59), in which I say that if English becomes an Indian language, it will be by stooping low to conquer, by losing its elitism. There has been a kind of lumpenization of English. It has become so vulgar; look, for example, at the use of a certain kind of demotic English by the characters in both Bhagat and Amish, who use four-letter words freely. But 'vulgar' also means 'common' in the old etymological sense. And in that sense we have to acknowledge that English has become an Indian language.

Sinha: This brings me to the next point. Through the help of translations, aren't we creating an alternative corpus of pan-Indian literatures in English?

Trivedi: I'm all for it, but there's another factor. The volume of literatures translated into Hindi is far more than what gets translated into English. A moment of revelation came when I went to attend the Jnanpith Award ceremony for Mahashweta Devi. She said that her works wouldn't have been known outside Bengal but for her translators and I thought she was going to mention her English translator, Gayatri Chakravorty Spivak. But she didn't. She said she was very grateful to Arvind Kumar, her Hindi translator and publisher who made her works known nationally. That is the ground reality! Bhalchandra Nemade is the latest Jnanpith winner, and the Hindi translation of his major recent novel *Hindu,* published in Marathi in 2013, is already available while the English version is yet to come. These facts should be better known to help dispel our blind reverence for English. Also, being confined to English is harming us. Many of us read only what is available in English. This is what colonization does, this is what globalization does.

Sinha: We also wanted to talk to you about the syllabus in the classroom. In 1999 you were instrumental in introducing a new kind of English literature syllabus in the DU classroom, a syllabus with a very large Indian component. You have also talked about your ideal of the 'Panchdhatu' syllabus. Nearly two decades later, how far do you think this 'experiment' if I may call it, has succeeded?

Trivedi: Well, it was a great thing to have happened but I also have mixed feelings about that. When I am talking to new people or am introduced to an audience, people mention this syllabus change as if it was my greatest achievement, and perhaps it was because nothing else that I have done has had such a widespread and long-lasting effect. Of course, I could do it only with widespread support from teachers from all colleges. I am delighted that it happened in a democratic fashion.

Sinha: I remember that there was so much enthusiasm at that time.

Trivedi: There was a kind of groundswell and a democratic longing for a change. I am very pleased with it and proud of the collective transformation that we were able to accomplish.

Sinha: I also remember a series of workshops that were held in 1999 regarding the new syllabus, with talks by Professor Sisir Kumar Das, Professor Namwar Singh and other scholars from Departments other than English. These workshops created a new generation of teachers who were tuned to the idea of teaching Indian literature in English translations in the English Department. It was so refreshingly different.

Trivedi: Exactly. But I also said I have mixed feelings about it. Let me tell you what Professor Sisir Kumar Das said to me at that time; he was the Tagore Professor in the Department of Modern Indian Languages. We were very close friends and he was my guru in a way. He asked me if I had foreseen the consequences of what I was doing. I gave him all the idealistic reasons: that the students of English would look at India differently and would look at English and the Indian languages differently, and that it would create a new generation of more enlightened literature students. And he said there may be another consequence, that a student who might have been motivated to read a text in Bengali might now read it in English translation. Also, such students of English would read one novel in Bengali or Hindi in translation, or some poems, and think that they know all about Bengali or Hindi literature!

I think this may have to some extent come about. There is a perception now that a teacher of English literature in Delhi University knows quite a lot about Indian literature too! On the other hand, in recent years, some of our English students having read Indian authors in translation in the BA and MA have gone on to do their MPhils and PhDs in Indian literature in translation or originally in the Indian languages.

Sinha: Do you think a separate department for Indian Literature should be set up?

Trivedi: I want a separate department for English Language Teaching. That will call the bluff of English Literature in India. I want English language-learning to be available in a cheap, functional and efficient manner. A minimal or middle-level skill is what most people want in India through learning English. Who wants to study Shakespeare so as to acquire a practical knowledge of the English language?

Sinha: What do you think of the teaching of English language in our classrooms at the college level?

Trivedi: I commend *FORTELL* for its focus on the teaching of English language. There was a golden moment in English-language teaching in India which got nipped in the bud. This was the CIEFL-effect in the 1970s-80s, when even our brightest teachers wanted to train in ELT. But now, while English teachers in our colleges still teach a huge component of English language, they only acknowledge the literature texts they teach. We are living a lie by teaching literature when the demand is for language.

So, right, English is an Indian language, and let's teach it, but let's not mix it up with high canonical English literature. It is true that literature and philosophy are the repositories of the highest form of expression in any language. But not everybody needs that day in and day out. We need courses in systematic language-teaching. And I am quite clear in my mind that language need not be taught through literature and hoary literary classics.

I believe in functional English, I believe in ELT, I believe in graded-vocabulary texts; that is the way forward. Also, let's accept that our English is Indian English. Let's accept that most people in the West will not readily understand us when some of us go there.

Shahnaaz: When you say Indian English, what exactly do you have in mind?

Trivedi: It is what is common between those Indians who are reasonably well educated and reasonably competent in English without any pretensions to being international. The trouble with Indian English is that then it stops being an international language. You can have it only one way, not both ways. It can be either Indian or global.

Some people say they want to learn English to go abroad, to go to America. That's another ball game. Look at our call centres. Everybody there, all of whom were smart English-medium boys and girls, had to be re-trained intensively in their accent and vocabulary for the first few weeks before the Americans could understand them. Let's not be too proud of our English. Indian English is what well educated Indians use and understand, and just that.

Shahnaaz: But that English has also come to us through the British who ruled over us.

Trivedi: Right, it is an evolution of what came to us long back, its transformation taking place over 150 or 200 years of local conditions. Try reading West Indian English, for example Braithwaite's poems, or the dialogues in Naipaul's *A House for Mr. Biswas,* or the novels by Achebe or Ngugi. You may feel it is 'wrong' English and comical. In so many ways our English seems similarly 'wrong' and funny to the British or the Americans who use it as their first language. If English is an Indian language, what shall we tell them is their language? And if we operate in a second language, can we escape being second-rate in all kinds of ways?

2

Dominance of English Creates a Cultural Distortion

Makarand R. Paranjape

Interviewed by Barun Kumar Mishra

Barun Kumar Mishra: It is often said that economic power brings literary power, so where do you see India in this light, particularly in terms of literary and non-literary writings in English that emerge from India?

Makarand R. Paranjape: No doubt, economic power is related to cultural power. The former is thought of as 'hard' and the latter as 'soft' power; combine them strategically and you get 'smart' power. But the two types of powers are related. You might even say that economic power comes from cultural power, so it is not only a unidirectional causality that we see here but something that is bi-directional multidirectional, one thing leading to the other.

I think that Indians have already exploited the economic resources of the English language, as indeed, they have its creative resources. So, what I expect now is greater expansion in the market of other Indian languages like Hindi, Bengali, Punjabi, Marathi, Tamil and so on. And this will, I hope, provide a counter balance to the dominance of English. For me the dominance of English creates a cultural distortion both

---

Revised version of the interview earlier published in *FORTELL* Issue No. 12 (September 2007).

in India and abroad and we the teachers of English need to be aware of it.

Mishra: Can we say that India is/or becoming a literary powerhouse?

Paranjape: Well, India has always been a literary powerhouse. It is not a new development. We have a literature which goes back to 5000 years. If you talk in terms of quality and quantity, the literature produced in India in these last 5000 years is certainty enough to rival, if not exceed, that of any other country or civilization in the world. But it is one thing to talk about having cultural and literary depth, and it is another thing to talk about marketability. So, if you are using global standards then India has a lot to catching up to do but the truth of the matter is that the literature that we have produced in our twenty or so major Indian languages in the last 600-700 years can rival the best in world. To that, of course, we need to add the literature produced in English in the last 150 years. Or earlier, the literature in Persian from the 12th century C.E. until the late 19th century C.E. If you also add the literature produced in Sanskrit, Pali, Prakrits, and so on, then frankly I don't know any geographical territory or country which can even come close to India.

Mishra: How do you see the representation of India in literature produced globally? How far has the image shifted from being the 'museum of the orient'? Have the writers of Indian origin helped to transform it and create a more realistic image of India?

Paranjape: I think these writers, especially the writers living abroad have both contributed to exoticisation of India and have also tried to correct it; so it's a contradictory situation. The slot vacated by the Anglo-Indian writers or writers from the West who wrote about the Orient is now been occupied by Indian writers living abroad. I would even call them the neo-orientalists or, as the new term designates them, re-Orientalists.

The peculiarity of Indian writing in English is that some of its most important writers live abroad. Expatriate literature dominates. Imagine the narrative of a whole sub-continent of a billion and a quarter people controlled and hegemonized by a handful of highly visible and promoted writers living abroad! This is the conundrum.

How it would be, to give you an example, if the majority of the best Chinese writers lived in America or in England? Wouldn't it create a very strange and anomalous situation? Or if the best American writers all lived in China or in India? At one time the greatest American writers made it a practice of going to Paris, but that situation lasted just about a couple of decades. Also, they went as Americans, as expats, to expand their horizons, so to speak. Europe was much cheaper and gave them pause to reflect and write about the United States. But with Indian writers, this is a growing problem. They prefer to live close to the centres of publication and power, which are in the West.

If we consider the totality of literature produced in the English language the world over, I think Indians are playing increasingly an important role. Some of the most important English writers have an Indian or South Asian connection. Among the contemporary writers: Salman Rushdie lives in America, Michael Ondatjee in Canada hails from Sri Lanka, and Rohinton Mistry comes from India, and in Malaysia, K.S. Maniam the most important English writer is of Indian origin. In Australia a lot of important English writers are from India, so my point is wherever English is spoken Indians have reached there. In Latin America, many of the English departments have Indian professors. Indians have reached or will reach wherever English has reached and they will play an important role in that area, though they were colonized by English first, now they are part of the empire of the English language.

But, gradually, when we will have many more of our own Amish Tripathis and Chetan Bhagats, the situation will change.

Expats will continue to write in English, but *desi* English writers will become more and more visible and important. We may, eventually, be able to wrest the narrative control of India back from non-Indians and expats.

Mishra: In the syllabi of schools and universities, one notices a shift from Eurocentric literature to Indian literature. Keeping this transition in mind, what kind of literature would you suggest? Where would one place folk tales and mythological tales regarding their 'truth value'? What are the kinds of values and morality that they impart?

Paranjape: People think that mythological stories are useless; I find such a view bordering on idiocy. In my opinion even history is like fiction. A 'fact' doesn't exist in isolation. If a fact is put into a chain of other information and stories are constructed out of it, you have a powerful narrative, which can shape discourse and public opinion. Moreover, imaginative literature has a lot of truth value. It may not be literally true, like when one someone says, 'Oh! Hanuman jumped across from Rameshwaram to Sri Lanka', it is unbelievable from a scientific point of view. But from the point of view of poetic truth, I think it is very much believable. Just as Rambo, Spiderman or X-Men are believable. Or any other story believable where the protagonists seems to accomplish totally impossible feats. Just as James Bond, who is never killed, but put into a death trap only to escape, is also believable. None of these are believable from the purely practical or scientific point of view. But they all have some artistic or entertainment value and you cannot judge literary works from the point of literal truth.

This idea goes back to the *Natyashastra*. When the Asuras saw themselves being defeated in the fight between the Devas and the Asuras, they destroyed the playhouse, beat up the director, and stopped the performance, Brahma had to intervene and tell them that theatre had not to be taken literally. Tomorrow we can have a play in which Devas may lose. No doubt, art is deeply connected with power structure and politics, but it is not identical to it, as sometimes the Marxists think.

Our literary heritage is very rich and these Jataka or Panchatantra tales are not just *Dant Katha*. They have high moral values, spiritual values, artistic values. Our stories teach wisdom, they teach Dharma.

Mishra: When why are people prejudiced when it comes to Indian mythology?

Paranjape: I think only the intellectual class is prejudiced. That is because they are not confident of our tradition, so we see a self-loathing here, which is more dangerous than prejudice from outside. But the basic point of your question is the shift towards Indian writing in English and I think we have to go farther, we should now be studying Indian literature in English translation or we should have a way in which we can study literature in our own languages and write criticism in English. So, we have to move much farther because we are a multilingual society and the model of education that we inherited is a monolingual model from the British.

Mishra: If we look at our model of teaching, language is taught through literature. And we have access to literatures from India, Africa, Australia among others, so what role does literature play in language teaching? Are there alternative ways of teaching language?

Paranjape: Yes, there are various perspectives on teaching language, but I believe that some people teach language without literature. You can teach grammar, you can teach composition and you can make people read the newspaper or use any other text to teach language. The idea of teaching language through literature comes from the premise that literature is enjoyable, but what happens often is that the literary text is simply read in bazaar notes format. So if *Othello* is prescribed, students will simply read a guidebook on *Othello*. These are some of the problems in the 'teaching language through literature' model.

I feel that literature is something to be enjoyed and appreciated in and by itself. It is important for people who are studying the language to study the literature too. Obviously there are linguistic benefits in doing that. But I don't think literature should be merely the means to an end; it should be an end in itself. Similarly I don't believe language should be a means to an end. Like everybody thinks that English should only be for 'communication'. Or for special purposes, for educational purposes, social purposes, and so on. I don't agree. If I am learning a language, I would like to learn the language for the sake of the language. Each language in a multilingual society has a different domain. You know, it would be ridiculous if you speak to your mother exclusively in English. Unless both of you are native speakers of English. But if your mother tongue is Hindi, why would you talk exclusively in English? In India, all these multitudinous dimensions of language have to be explored and exploited. As Amitav Ghosh once told me, people want to read his works because they find other languages behind the English! It's what makes the creativity of a multilingual writer more interesting than a monolingual one.

Ultimately, however, as Bhartrihari would say, there is only one language which is human language. Maybe Chomsky would also agree that these many languages are all varieties of human language. English, Hindi, Chinese, Japanese, or whatever tongue you voice—these are all human language. So, I think human language is a vast ocean or creative possibility. One of the things that makes us human and distinguishes us from animals is language, and language is not a means to an end; it is an end in itself.

Mishra: You suggested that English for communication makes little sense, but proficiency in the language without, any knowledge of literature gets people jobs. In which case why should we not teach English language in place of English literature?

Paranjape: I think we all know the uses of English in India. Who can dispute that? If you want a job in a call centre you don't have to be taught literature. Language training and pronunciation coaching should be sufficient.

I don't think we need to teach English literature everywhere we teach English. In fact, there should be fewer literature departments, but they should really be excellent. You know what universities failed to do, private software institutes did for computer programming. Similarly, all the private English institutes are doing what we have not been able to deliver through universities. So we have to change our model and we should have many vocational and practical courses like Business English, English Communication, Technical English or English for sales, etc. These courses would help people land jobs and literature should be left for fewer people who are really deeply interested in it.

3

Need to be Conscious and Cautious of Learning from Other Disciplines

G.J.V. Prasad

Interviewed by Rachna Sethi

Rachna Sethi: Interdisciplinarity seems to be among one of the new directions that academia is moving towards in India. Yet there seems to be lack of clarity in defining the term itself. It is often confused with multidisciplinarity and transdisciplinarity. How does one differentiate between these terms?

G.J.V. Prasad: I agree there is a lot of confusion about the term interdisciplinarity. JNU was conceptualized as a university that would foster interdisciplinarity. When we began, technology was not that advanced and physical proximity of departments helped. One should of course have the orientation to want to converse with other disciplines for interdisciplinarity to work and physical nearness aids dialogue between disciplines. I would often run into other literary scholars, historians and sociologists like Namwar Singh, Anil Bhatti, Kalgare and Kedar Nath Singh. Meetings and discussions with social scientists and scholars from other languages over tea fostered interdisciplinarity at JNU.

And I am talking of 'inter' and not 'trans', that is disciplines talking to each other and working with each other.

Earlier published in *FORTELL* Issue No. 28 (January 2014).

That is how I have co-guided PhD scholars with historians; in interdisciplinary research projects one felt that the student needed inputs and methodologies of other disciplines. In transdisciplinarity you do not feel the need to learn the discipline of each field. Multidisciplinary depends on your training, if you are actually trained or inclined to train in two or more disciplines. A colleague of mine studied English with me, followed it by study of History and now teaches in the Political Science Department, I would call him a truly multidisciplinary person. Otherwise we have people from different fields coming together in collaborations, providing opportunities for different disciplines to converse and create a new discursive space.

Sethi: The physical proximity between departments seems to be a thing of the past with the growth of JNU. Perhaps now informal discussions over tea are being replaced by formal networks of exchanges. How do you see the change in dynamics reflect on interdisciplinarity?

Prasad: The change in atmosphere means that today we need networks to encourage interdisciplinarity. Apart from research projects, certain programmes on campus like the North East India Studies programme and sector for education require expertise from different departments.

Also one notices an interdisciplinary and transdisciplinary push not just in JNU but across the country by policy makers. The ministry has picked up these terms and there may be more funding and opportunities for younger colleagues in interdisciplinary areas. Today there is no funding in universities for Humanities but some for Social Sciences and that is also the reason for more collaborative seminars and research projects.

Sethi: Interdisciplinarity is often viewed as being central to reading and understanding of literature. What is the direction that English Studies has taken in India in view of academic needs of crossing disciplinary boundaries?

Prasad: English departments, along with perhaps History and Sociology to some extent, are unique in understanding the fuzziness of boundaries. English departments in India could have gone in two possible directions. One way would have been to specialize in language teaching, to teach English as a language that will be useful to participate in the wider affairs of the world and as a link language across India. However this has not been very successful as language teaching is often looked down upon in universities. A hierarchy prioritizing literature over language exists in university spaces.

The second direction that English departments could have taken was to explore the 'Englishness', to see our departments as simply literary studies departments but again this did not happen. For a very long time we remained very 'English' and never became literature departments, and then we moved away from being English departments to becoming Cultural Studies departments. This is the manner in which most literature departments have reinvented themselves. We seem to have skipped the Literary Studies phase and fast forwarded to the Cultural Studies phase and boundaries automatically became fuzzy.

In Cultural Studies you are dealing with everything from History to Political Science to Linguistics to Translation Studies to Cinema Studies. Interestingly Indian languages, which had been neglected in English departments, were co-opted in this Cultural Studies phase. Study of popular and cultural forms brought in study of Indian languages and literature and you could now study Hindi or Tamil literature in an English department without raising eyebrows. Indian literature has gained entry into English departments because of the need to re-present Indian culture, to analyse India and to create a critical discourse on India.

Sethi: So Cultural Studies has not only dismantled the study of the British literary canon but also blurred disciplinary boundaries in English departments.

Prasad: The fuzziness of borders between disciplines is now part of the turf of English departments. Interdisciplinarity earlier meant that you should be totally conversant with methodologies of other disciplines but that is no longer demanded. It has its own pros and cons. It is good in the sense that it has made English departments exciting places to be in and bad because humility and admittance of lack of knowledge about other disciplines has been replaced by brashness. One needs to question the training of students in other disciplines when we don't even train people any longer in close reading of texts.

Sethi: Teaching of literature has always involved drawing from disciplines of History, Philosophy, Sociology and Psychology even before we widely started using the term interdisciplinarity. Do you think there is a pedagogical shift in the current scenario in dealing with other disciplines?

Prasad: The difference between then and now is being able to speak of other disciplines with a sense of ease, sometimes even contemptuously. We were actually trained by historians and History just didn't come into the literature class. When we attended History and Philosophy classes we had a sense that these were aligned disciplines but different disciplines nonetheless. Literary Studies always had interdisciplinarity, now I think there is a feeling that you don't need to learn History from historians, Psychology from psychologists, Philosophy from philosophers, as if the literary scholar is all in one.

Sethi: It seems that instead of improving on skills, one is drawing from multiple disciplines without being trained in them. Don't you feel that the biggest drawback of interdisciplinarity is lack of grounding in any discipline while trying to be 'a jack of all trades'?

Prasad: Yes, that is a problem. When you hear and read people with firm grounding in a discipline, a literary scholar who knows his text well, you value his merit as an intellectual and critic. I don't want to sound old fashioned because I love this excitement and enjoy the kind of research young scholars can undertake today. However we need to be conscious and cautious of learning from other disciplines and not pick up ideas without being aware of where they come from.

Sethi: Interdisciplinarity then shouldn't lead to a superficial research that lacks substance and depth.

Prasad: Absolutely, also since our work is part of the literature department, our reading of literature should be central to what we do, otherwise it is just a peg to hang other things. Otherwise the same kind of work can possibly be done in a History or a Sociology department.

Sethi: You are suggesting that we make literature central to our project in the English department and then use tools of other disciplines. But how do we ensure that these tools are used for synthesis of ideas, for advancement of knowledge? What methodology should the teacher employ to equip students in interdisciplinary work?

Prasad: Let me push it further, today I have a tool kit rather than methodologies that I provide my students with. The tools may come from different disciplines, drawing from what I have learnt from these streams over the years. I fail in my responsibility as a teacher if I don't train my students in understanding the functions and impacts of tools and how they are to be used for analysis of texts. They should be able to decide the appropriate tool for the unpacking or decoding of a text. Research Methodology is about putting a tool kit together. As I said earlier, it doesn't mean you lose humility and pretend or think that you know all, but instead you learn and evolve and have respect for different tools that you have gained. In that sense it doesn't matter if you are not trained in different disciplines so long as you are familiar with different tools, know their origins and various uses.

Sethi: Has the JNU administration been supportive of partnership among departments for research proposals based on interdisciplinary approach? Can you please give examples of such joint ventures undertaken at the Centre for English Studies?

Prasad: JNU has always been supportive in having co-supervisors not only from other departments but also from other universities in India or even abroad. We are open to being in the liminal space between disciplines and encourage crossing of boundaries.

I can give you examples of PhD research of Ramya Sreenivasan and Nilanjana Mukherjee. Both had projects that were heavily History-oriented, and had co-supervisors from History departments and their theses have been appreciated by people from History and Literature departments. I have also supervised work where students have worked on other Indian languages like Tamil and Bengali and that work has been appreciated by people from those respective languages, and that was a test for me.

4

Genre Fluidity Will Make its Own Space

Christel R. Devadawson

Interviewed by Rachna Sethi

Rachna Sethi: Let's begin by plunging into the debate about the Nobel Prize for Literature being awarded to Bob Dylan recently. Is it a reflection of the expanding and dynamic definition(s) of literature?

Christel R. Devadawson: I think the Nobel Prize like a great deal of other international awards is meant primarily to raise awareness and build consciousness along lines of thought that appear revolutionary. If we are looking at revolution of the literary space, then one would have problems. At the same time it is a very valuable kind of gesture. By focusing on the 1960s, which is a watershed time in the formation of public opinion, it tells us a great deal about individuals, where their thoughts and struggles demolish and alter public institutions, including the government institutions that Dylan writes/ sings about, and also impacting different sites of institutional authority including universities. So I am very happy that this kind of work is recognized.

And if the Nobel [Prize] is one way of reminding us that these were ideas that we have let go and have tended to forget, then I would say it is justified. We need to think of literature beyond its textual definition. My own sense is that if the arts are to evolve, if they are to remain continually relevant to

Earlier published in *FORTELL* Issue No. 34 (January 2017).

society, then they must engage with revolution, on the ground and in terms of structure. And when you think of the kind of changes that Dylan's work seeks to address; they carry a sense of engagement, a need for change, and place the individual as the parameter of the social and the cultural.

Sethi: While the idea of literature and revolution works on the thematic concerns, let us focus on the formalistic aspects of literature. Considering the interest of the students in genres like blog writing, graffiti art, films, cartoons and graphic novels, are we moving towards genre fluidity? Are the boundaries of the discipline being pushed and expanded towards Cultural Studies?

Devadawson: Genre fluidity is an integral part of human activity, we may engage with it in the classroom or not, but it will exist, and it will be foolish of us not to engage with it as it will make changes in the world on its own terms. So the better idea is for us to engage with it in the classroom. Having said that, it will make its own space and win its own battles.

I think Cultural Studies will always be an immensely exciting phase through which the discipline moves but I would say that the imperative term here is 'moving'. We are moving through a much more fluid and far more open-ended space and we need to engage with a new kind of globalization, not the globalization that was feared as a great public enemy some time ago, but a certain kind of a very broad and complicated cultural space through which we must negotiate.

Sethi: What changes does this new kind of globalization bring to university spaces and structures? Does it necessitate new curriculum, pedagogical practices and evaluation systems? Ideally this should not be a linear process but a back and forth engagement, the examination pattern requiring a new pedagogical approach. However the purpose of a revised syllabus is often defeated if the questions continue to be traditional in nature and non-challenging. Should the fluidity not flow from syllabus to evaluation?

Devadawson: I agree, but I think that the critical component that we need to look at in the march that we have taken is the student, even though syllabi and exams have vital roles to play as you have pointed out. The keystone in the academic arch will be and always has been the student in the classroom. We have to admit that with the passage of time, there have been many valuable and altering shifts in the definition of who constitutes the student in the classroom. We need to address who is the student, what would the student benefit from or take away by engaging say with English Studies rather than another discipline, and what would be the role of the syllabus for the student, will it provide a floor or a ceiling? All of us need to think and talk about this, and people will think differently about these variables, but I would repeat that in these critical variables, the student is the most important keystone. We need to look at the definitions of the discipline, the role of syllabus and examination, and we need to look at them in terms of an evolving discipline and an evolving student or evolving ways of student life.

Sethi: Let me give an example of the disjunction between syllabus and evaluation. Some colleagues felt that if the question paper skirts around the queer aspect of Shyam Selvadurai's *Funny Boy*, it in some ways defeats the purpose of including it in a revised syllabus. Why should the exam paper ignore that vital aspect?

Devadawson: When we included Selavdurai's *Funny Boy* in the syllabus, the other text we had in mind was Mahesh Dattani's *Dance Like a Man*, and we chose the former. We ultimately went with *Funny Boy* because we felt that in it Selvadurai captures a particular moment of performative change in the self, the national self and also the sexualized self, or rather the self that is in the process of sexualizing and socializing. When this was discussed, some of our colleagues expressed concern about how many of these performative, socializing, nationalizing, sexualizing changes could be taken on board by students from very different backgrounds. It is possible that the exam paper seeks to address what I would call the common denominator; not so much the specialized notions but generalized notions, of say society, national change and the self. I would be sorry to think of an examination system that wipes out completely the question of performative sexuality. If an examiner thinks of that question but does not include it, I would be sorry, but I would be sympathetic. I would be much more critical of an MPhil course if it wiped out this question, and we have had *Funny Boy* as part of a course earlier. But with a first year undergraduate student, if the examiner tells me the limitations of how much an exam paper can address, I would be sorry but I will understand. If it comes to push or shove, I would say, better that the text is taught and examined partially rather than an area of literary concern not dealt with.

Sethi: Approach(es) to texts vary as you have just pointed out, from BA to say MPhil, and would bring about a corollary difference in the quality of writing expected. Students write assignments and tests right from school to college, and yet writing as a process is rarely addressed. At what grade/level do you think its formal aspects should be addressed?

Devadawson: I think the moment one begins to shape letters, some component of writing has to be introduced, and generally is introduced in school. I think at the undergraduate level, it will be a good idea to look at the basics of academic writing, the use of work of other scholars, quarrelling with works of other scholars, quarrelling with one's own work, placing texts in contexts, placing texts in history; I think these basics can be and should be discussed.

Can we ever talk in terms of a separate component [of writing] within the syllabus, I am not sure about that. And the reason I am not sure is because the size of the class varies widely in our university. It would be more feasible in a relatively smaller college/university, which has a good student-teacher ratio. While we are aware of the UGC guidelines of the student-teacher ratio, we know that in the reality of bargaining of posts, these ratios are not followed. While I realize the need for these [writing skills] to be taught and to be examined separately, I bow to the good sense of my colleagues in colleges who tell me that these are unrealistic requirements; and that is how the notion of not just the internal assessment but continuous assessment is excellent in terms of concept and theory, but it is very difficult to manage on the ground.

Sethi: Now we have a Generic Elective (GE) paper on 'Academic Writing and Composition' at the undergraduate level in DU, and you have just pointed the practical difficulties of executing it. In an ideal scenario, editing and revising are integral to the process of writing. Do you think only a workshop format will make it more feasible rather than a classroom?

Devadawson: Or a tutorial format, where the student-teacher ratio is favourable, but I am aware it can be viewed as elitist. That kind of arithmetic does not always translate into either a pedagogical proficiency or social responsibility.

Sethi: So revising, which is central to writing, is an issue that is not addressed probably till the time one comes to a research programme like the MPhil, as the immense size of the MA classroom is daunting.

Devadawson: With the Masters, internal assessment attempts to take care of this difficulty, of course it does not deal with it satisfactorily, nothing ever does. In fact, even when we come to the MPhil, we do have the pressure not just of numbers but of timelines, and research continues to be affected by it. Most MPhil students go on to teach, and of course they want to be independent, and that makes it difficult. If the timelines are rigid and have to be kept, then perhaps one needs to wipe out other concerns like taking care of funding.

Sethi: Apart from 'Academic Writing and Composition' CBCS has also introduced a Skill Enhancement Course (SEC) on 'Creative Writing'. How do you respond to the idea that creativity is inherent, you are born a dancer and can't be taught to be one? Or is creativity a craft that can be taught?

Devadawson: True, but you can be taught about the discipline of dance and that is where the teaching component comes in. You can be taught to write, say fiction. We might have courses where at the end we have more rather than less competent writers of fiction. Most of the creative writing programmes, say in the United States, rely on guest and visiting faculty, and that makes it possible to offer these courses, and they are generally offered as non-credit courses, and I imagine it would be very difficult to manage that within Delhi University. We had an experience once at South Campus where we had a poet in residence, Keki N. Daruwalla. He was very generous, very forthcoming, read students' poetry but it was not something that can be done on a broader scale.

Sethi: Do you think one needs creative writers to conduct creative writing courses?

Devadawson: I find it difficult to say, since I haven't tried it. I think my attitude would be somewhat old-fashioned and somewhat sceptical. I recall Narayan's idea in *The Vendor of Sweets* where Mali goes to the United States to undertake a creative writing course. Mine is not a position of opposition but of concern about these courses.

Sethi: Stylistically one can discuss and teach different aspects of writing, but what about the language aspect? The language of young people today is heavily influenced by social media, and while we keep it outside the formal exam-writing with great difficulty, the 'lingo' is bound to infiltrate creative writing. Can we or should we even hold onto purist notions of language?

Devadawson: Language change will come about, no matter what. It will storm into examination halls, into media, our personal space, whether or not we approve of it. I think it is not so much whether we allow it to or not, but how we decide to negotiate it, how we decide to mediate it, to talk about it, and let's face it to enjoy it. One needs to be much more open-ended in terms of ideas of what constitutes intellectual enjoyment. And I would return to your earlier question about Dylan and one of his critics Christopher Ricks, who has made a name by writing about Milton, but his enjoyment and critical appreciation of Milton does not dent his enjoyment and critical appreciation of Dylan. We need to have fun and be more tolerant about what constitutes literature within universities.

Sethi: Dylan brings us back to stretchable boundaries of literature and fluidity of genres. Forms like blogs, vlogs and photo essays are very popular with the students; where would one locate them when dealing with Academic Writing and Creative Writing?

Devadawson: With Creative Writing, they will storm in, no matter what. With Academic Writing, it is about how much time the student has and there are conferences being held on various kinds of writing. The question is not whether we will allow it, the question is how much time the young have where we have expectations of them, and depending on what is culturally and commercially valuable, and this is the direction in which this argument should be pushed in future.

Pedagogical Challenges

5

Fluidity Constitutes the Core of Multilinguality

Rama Kant Agnihotri

Interviewed by Barun Kumar Mishra

Barun Kumar Mishra: What we gather from the policy decision of the state and its various agencies regarding language teaching is that a greater emphasis is given to a simultaneous teaching of English language and the mother tongue. First, I would be interested to know whether the approach taken to teach is bridging the social gap or widening it further. Second, what do you mean by mother tongue education when there is a difference between regional language and mother tongue? For example, Bundelkand region has two languages, Bundeli and Hindi.

Rama Kant Agnihotri: I think we need to understand three important things before we get into these issues. First is the nature of language; the second concerns the human mind and language; and the third is concerned with the relationship between language, mind and society. So, let's take language first. For the people in power, the concept of 'a language' is sacred; most linguists, literary scholars, institutions which give them awards, the politicians who decide to fight for a new state or a nation, or the school, college and university teachers, treat

Updated version of the interview earlier published in *FORTELL* Issue No. 8 (April 2006).

language as a rarefied homogeneous object. It is a systematic pairing of a lexicon and a set of syntactic structures; it must be codified through grammars and dictionaries and a large range of reference books. Its normative standard must not be violated in speech or writing.

The linguistic behaviour of common people is very different. They are powerless; so are their languages. If you look at the language of the material world i.e. the language of movies, hoardings and advertisements, people talking at home or on the street, of peer group interactions and festivals and weddings, it is very different; it is fluid. It is a verbal repertoire where a whole range of 'languages' effortlessly flow into each other. The first issue then is that the concept of 'a language' is not viable; not valid. So we need to think about human language capacity, which should be defined as multilinguality. Whether a human being speaks one language or two languages or whether she or he speaks five or six languages, is not the point; the point is even if you think you are a monolingual, you actually are not a monolingual. You fine tune your linguistic behaviour all the time, and that the capacity to fine tune linguistic behaviour is called multilinguality. Coming to the issue of language and the human mind, the only convincing hypothesis we have is that the human mind is genetically endowed with a Language Faculty, a faculty that is unique and distinct from other cognitive faculties. This Language Faculty enables people, particularly young children till the age of about fourteen, to acquire many languages at the same time. They have greater flexibility, they acquire languages with greater ease, particularly the oral skills, pronunciation, communicative proficiency. The Language Faculty always remains there, but not as flexible as at the younger age. Young children of three or four years of age can speak three or four languages without any difficulty. Fortunately, there is democracy there and also it has nothing to do with how rich or poor you are. Students would be speaking Bhojpuri at home, Hindi with friends and English at their colleges. I think it is an important dimension to appreciate for all those who are interested in the education of the underprivileged sections of society. For the people who are seriously interested in bridging the gulf between the rich and the poor, I think, it is imperative to understand that every child irrespective of his or her background has the capacity to acquire several languages. So if your child starts speaking three languages you don't take your child to a hospital. The human mind has that capacity and I characterize it as multilinguality. There is always a range there and you keep moving around that range, depending on who you are talking to, where you are talking and about what you are talking. That takes us to the issues of Language, Mind and Society; we could distinguish between a dominating multilinguality of the elite and a dominated multilinguality of the masses. I think the agenda of education is to ensure voices of the dominated multilinguality a place that is due to them. At the intersection of empowered and powerless languages would appear subversive spaces.

Mishra: Would you say that knowledge of language is a part of the child's consciousness?

Agnihotri: That is a difficult question. We do not know to what extent this knowledge is conscious. This may be deeply subconscious but the empirical demonstration is there all the time because a four year old child knows exactly whom to address as *aap, tum* and *tuu*. He or she doesn't make a mistake there. Nor does he/she make a mistake in the use of grammar because the grammar of using the second person honorific *aap* is very different from the grammar of using the non-honorific *tum* or *tuu*. He/she does not consciously know this, and cannot tell the rules. For that matter, adults do not know the grammatical rules either. What grammar books tell you is very limited, finite, and actually trivial, as compared to what we really know in the subconsciousness. This serious business of *aap, tum* and *tuu* brings me again to the third point. Once this point about the Language Faculty is well taken, then the ability to use language creatively in the social context is acquired. There is a strong relationship between language and context. You use not only grammatically correct language, but also contextually appropriate language. Every grammar has a universal core which is related to the Language Faculty, but every language also has its specificities. Every language variety is a phenomenon in itself because politeness strategies and cultural associations are different and so on. And that is acquired in a social set-up. It is not innate, that is why society is so important. Now given all this, what we notice is that the gulf between the underprivileged, and the small section of the elite and the powerful, is consistently widening. When we refer back to our commitments in the Constitution the objective there is to narrow down the gulf and work for the empowerment of the poor people.

Mishra: You mean the foundational objectives of the welfare state?

Agnihotri: Yes, all these things were conceptualized—free education, free shelter, free health, water—all this you know was seen as the responsibility of the state there. It was expected that everybody will have easy access to all of them; irrespective of who the learner is, the quality of education will not be compromised; nor the principle of inclusion trivialized. And I think we did make a positive beginning. There was a time when the free schools were quite good, even better than the ones that were privately managed (public schools). The honourable thing to do till the 1960s was to go to a government school. Though it reached only the lower and middle classes, the system of government healthcare and sanitation appeared to be on the right track and it seemed reasonable to dream that we would be able to fulfil the promises made in the Constitution for all. All of us have studied in government schools. But since then the situation has become worse. There may be many reasons for that—social, political and economic. But one of the major factors has been the English language; depriving the underprivileged and keeping them away from the English language which provides you access to power, social mobility, employment, jobs of all kinds. This has been done in various ways. First, all elite children would start English from the kindergarten and all underprivileged children would start from Class 6. English teachers were not appointed. Many states, in their enthusiasm for Hindi, declared that all work would be done in Hindi. You could actually do your schooling without English. It was very good for people to pass without English, but when they came into society, into colleges, in the universities, they felt handicapped. Many people studied almost exclusively in Hindi and other regional languages. There is nothing wrong with that. In fact, it has helped several regional languages to become richer. But this does not justify keeping the underprivileged away from English, given that the way we constructed our society, English provided the main access to jobs and social mobility. At the end of the road, several highly educated and intelligent people found they could not get decent jobs. So it is against this background that I think of the National Curriculum Framework (NCF 2005). Both the position papers on the teaching of Indian languages and the position papers on the teaching of English, very strongly admit that if, and that is the big **IF**, that if one can make suitable arrangements for teaching-learning materials, for teacher training, and for schools and teachers—then every child must have access to English as early as possible. And this is not going to harm; what harms is that you introduce English in Class 1 but provide no infrastructure, teachers, textbooks or materials. That creates a situation which is absolutely undesirable. The Court mandates 25 per cent reservation for economically weaker sections in private schools, and studies show that those children did better than, or certainly as well as other children. So, there is nothing wrong with the children. The state has withdrawn its hands from the notion of a welfare state, so it will have to introduce English and it will have to provide resources that are necessary to introduce English. Teacher training is an important part of it—library books, teaching-learning material, all this should be provided. And it is eminently doable. All our college and university teachers are products of government schools and colleges, then why not now? What has gone wrong? Note that I am not recommending the promotion of English at the cost of the languages of learners; that would militate against the basic grain of multilinguality. Learners should be able to acquire high levels of proficiency in at least three or four languages. Note that in the course of learning these languages, learners would often 'mix' languages; that's natural and should be encouraged. Fluidity constitutes the core of multilinguality; historically, that's the way all languages came into being. There has been an increase in population, in the number of teachers, there is no shortage of basic facilities; we grow enough food, build houses, build flyovers and metros, then why not provide poor people with education, healthcare and work? Why can't we have a common school? I think that is the most rational question to ask, why is there not the same kind of school in every street? Why should a five year old child travel 40 kilometres in a bus to go to school? Why should there be a school that is so different from an ordinary school? I think a common school is the first battle to be fought. And given these things, there should be no problem in that.

Mishra: Do you feel that the simultaneous knowledge/ teaching of English and mother tongue would be desirable?

Agnihotri: It is now well established that there is a positive correlation between multilingualism and scholastic achievement. That means that the higher the degree of proficiency in different languages, the higher is the achievement in different subjects. The purpose of our education should not be to introduce English only but to enhance high levels of proficiency in the mother tongue and the languages of the region. If we use our resources carefully then we can build high levels of proficiency in three or four languages by the time the child passes Class 12. While doing your elementary

English if you are doing your high levels in your regional languages, then, as studies show, those high level skills of regional languages—like writing an abstract essay, or logical argumentation—are transferable from one language to the other and help the learner to develop the other languages. So, automatically, English language proficiency will go up and will go up with multilinguality not with some crafted monolingualism. That is the emphasis of the National Curriculum Framework 2005.

Mishra: As you mentioned there been a political will to stop the introduction of English, and a section still considers English 'foreign' despite its significance in social life. What would you say about the academic debate over Indian English?

Agnihotri: There is no denying that English was brought to India by the British during colonial times. But you see all languages come from somewhere. So, I do not think that it is a very strong argument, more so because now English is no longer a foreign language for India except in rural areas. We have to consider English not only as a second language but in fact, as one of the languages of India. It has become so much a part of the ambience, certainly the urban ambience, it is part of mass media, judiciary, corporate world, academics—it is here and not likely to go away. It does differ from other varieties of English in pronunciation and some domains of lexicon. But that is certainly true of all varieties of English. At the level of core syntactic structures, English spoken by fluent users is no different from any other variety. And my question is, why should we let it go? Even for the concept of multilinguality we must ensure that English should not flourish at the cost of our regional languages. It is conceivable and desirable that English stays along with the other languages and they enrich one another. English does not close its doors; if you look at the Oxford English Dictionary, every year they add an annexure. It is very difficult to eliminate the concept of 'a language' from the minds of people. People keep quarrelling over the words, whether it belongs to that particular language used by its user, or not. This fight is actually on. These stereotypes travel from one generation to the next generation. It is simply a question of time and of the level of development that language has achieved. Words travel, they do not need passports like humans. Public interaction enriches languages; they borrow words from each other, assimilate them and make them their own. We need to have a fluid approach to language.

Mishra: Is the over emphasis on English causing a linguistic imbalance? There are constitutional provisions to safeguard the mother-tongue at elementary level and English is seen by people as replacing regional languages from their position. What are your views about this?

Agnihotri: The National Curriculum Framework 2005, which is now the guiding light for the future, has accepted and very strongly recommended most of the things discussed so far. Throughout the documents, as far as the languages are concerned, there is very strong emphasis on the mother tongue as the medium of instruction. In fact, we have gone to the extent of saying that the medium of instruction must be the mother tongue. We have laid a lot of emphasis on the mother tongue, trying to capitalize on multilingualism in the classroom as a resource. Not as an obstacle but as a teaching strategy, and also as a goal suggesting that it is something that should be sustained. It is possible to plan pedagogy particularly in a primary school where a child comes with two or three languages. For example, a *Saura* tribe child may know three languages, *Saura*, Oriya and some Hindi. This is the individual case. As a community, one particular class knows many languages. So, the teacher has to see that linguistic behaviour as a resource, and build it into their curriculum, syllabi and their day-to-day teaching. There is another important aspect to it, which is very fundamental and which I have been trying to argue for a long time. If you insult or humiliate the languages of the child in the classroom then his or her educational career comes to a stop that day; he/she would stop coming to the school. It hurts if somebody insults your mother tongue. So it should also be a necessary part of teacher training that teachers are made aware that all languages, irrespective of whether they are called dialect, *dehati* or *khichri*, are equally rich grammatically. That kind of awareness has to be there among the teachers. In order to prove this, language data should be elicited from students, teachers should become learners and also realize that they do not have to deposit knowledge in empty vessels. Even a preliminary analysis of that data would show the richness and grammaticality of the languages learners bring from home. Since children themselves are very creative, teachers should play the role of a facilitator. There is a whole social dynamic within the classroom. Unless a teacher is sensitive to these things, he/she may not be able to enrich that class. That kind of training is absolutely necessary. And I am not talking about something utopian, it is very practical. One can select a poem from, let's say, *Chhattisgarh* or *Saura* language, and ask some child who knows the language to translate it for the class. Since the teacher himself/herself does not know the language, he/she should sit at the back of the class. He/she is not the hero-teacher there who knows everything, he/she is a student; the poem is recited, its meaning is understood; then the class is split into different groups and students are asked to translate it into their mother tongues. Students are forbidden to borrow words and expressions from other languages they know. There is extensive language activity and language learning there.

Mishra: Considering the role of socio-economic factors, how can high levels of proficiency be achieved by a child born and brought up in a village? What changes should be made at policy level since mere change of syllabi has not done anything considerable so far?

Agnihotri: Yes, I agree with you that simply a change of syllabus, or changes in textbooks and materials will not deliver the goods. What we need to do is to conceptualize a total comprehensive intervention system. First of all, sufficient budget should be provided (which governments are refusing to give. Even the promised budget has never come). Everything should be taken as a comprehensive unit, where one should start with aims of education, their philosophical underpinnings, the curriculum, the syllabi, the textbooks, teacher training, school management, interaction with the community, etc. Teacher-training should be a lifetime process. If teachers are not constantly enriched, how can they enrich the students? If you want to enrich teachers, cluster resource centres and block resource centres should be activated. Schools should have a building with toilets, particularly for girls. We have seen girls drop out from schools in the absence of such facilities. There should be a bigger central reference library at the block level. College and university teachers should constantly interact with the school teachers at the block level, so that there is a dialogue. There are nearly eight thousand teachers in Delhi University but hardly any interact with schools. Since one is going to teach the same students, he/she should be aware of what is going on there, so that they can contribute better. It should be obligatory for every college/university teacher to visit a school once or twice a week and spend at least two hours there. When I say the totality has to be examined, things of that kind should be taken into account. Once again it is very much possible.

Mishra: Every language has a syntax and morphology, and given the condition of limited resources and infrastructure, what kind of linguistic linguistic competency can be expected from the learners? We are also faced with a situation where the instructors themselves are not linguistically proficient.

Agnihotri: I have already answered the latter part that teacher enrichment programme should be our first priority. The problem has arisen because of the missing conceptual machinery that is needed for a discipline. Therefore, the teachers could not generate interest among the students. It is not that students are inherently incompetent. Regarding language structures, I want to say that of course different languages have different structures, phonotactic rules, different morphological systems, but the real depth of those systems are not known to teachers or teacher trainers or parents. There is no question of teaching that, we cannot, what is taught in the name of grammar in schools is patently wrong. For example, 'an' is used before vowel letters, 'a' is used before consonants—this is wrong. You have to explain to the child why 'a' is used before a consonantal sound because there is a great difference between a consonantal letter and a consonantal sound. If you ask any teacher of English about the difference between a consonantal sound and a vocalic sound it will be hard for him/her to explain. English plural is not made by adding an—s, -es or -ies. Those are issues of writing. People who never go to schools and never write anything also make plurals; language in that sense is speech. Languages are not acquired by teaching language rules and grammar. Languages, on the other hand, are acquired by putting children in a kind of environment which is interesting, challenging, and where you have rich comprehensible input. They have the language faculty to abstract the rules.

6

A Text can Come Alive for and Through the Child in the Classroom

Rimli Bhattacharya

Interviewed by Barun Kumar Mishra

Barun Kumar Mishra: What according to you are the texts and themes appropriate for children's literature?

Rimli Bhattacharya: Before we discuss the themes, we should first ask who defines what 'children's literature' is. We might begin by saying that whatever children read, or whatever stories that children listen to, or are exposed to, through performance, oral narration, visual illustration or films or music or anything—that becomes a constituent element of children's literature at a particular moment. I'm not going into the whole history of the construction of childhood in different cultures. As for the themes, the assumption is that there is a body of people or institutions, organizations, who actually determine what is 'acceptable' for children and therefore influence what themes will get into the circuit. But of course, it doesn't always work like that. Traditionally too, this has been a matter of debate. Say, when the Brothers Grimm collected folk tales in the second volume, the revised edition, they had to delete/edit a lot of what had already been put in the first. So it seems that there was a contradiction between what they thought as an 'authentic' collection of folk tales and what was considered 'suitable' for children's literature.

Earlier published in *FORTELL* Issue No. 9 (August 2006).

Mishra: So, the debate about children's literature and the suitability of themes is an old one.

Bhattacharya: Yes, now here come very many questions. If you take up the question of violence, then what kind of violence can children be exposed to? Should you have adult themes, for example? Now we have all sorts of new categories in terms of age and degrees of violence. But on the other side, we live in a much harsher world which is not as protected, so you cannot continue with old models. There is also an ethical dimension, which may or may not get translated into the production of moral tracts. And increasingly, there is a third dimension, not much discussed in India—which is the whole question of what the market decides is suitable for children. It is the market that decides that this or that particular brand of biscuits is going to be made the child's favourite. There is a very conscious decision taken and it is implemented.

Since the forces of the market are so strong and pervasive and global, they have a tremendous reach in deciding what is that category called 'children' and why or how product 'X' is suitable for children. So you cannot look at the viability of themes in literature for children in isolation. You have to see it in a larger context, that's why I give the examples of soft drinks, biscuits or pizzas. One aspect of contemporary globalization is that it turns everything from poetry or pizza into a product, before it has had time to be produced, as it were.

Mishra: How do you envisage the role of media? How does it affect children, at the level of family life and at school?

Bhattacharya: These are actually very large questions, and I will address some. Tying up your earlier question with this one, clearly there is a link between the way media works and what children will finally end up reading; i.e. those children who will learn to read or have the time and money to read thereafter. Advertising is not only telling us how we should live, but also I think it is more insidiously presenting itself as life, mediating it through specific sets of images. So it is not just the prescriptive pressure of how one should live, but also a matter of how it works on the child's sensibility. All literature —and particularly children's literature— and of course, when I say literature it could include painting, a range of visual and performative arts—all of it actually in the case of children, should nurture something that is growing. What is happening in fact is that all those spaces are being blocked off, not only by one or the other message, but also by the mode in which the message is presented. So any sensitivity to language and differences in speech and sounds, the nuances of irony and humour—everything is increasingly getting wiped out. There is a homogenization happening. And people who are nativist might argue that this is happening only in case of English; therefore let the children read Hindi, Bangla or any other Indian language. My argument would be that in many cases the so-called authentic 'native' languages are doing the same thing, much more unconsciously, and therefore much more insidiously. So the danger of media cannot be put in a general way, that everything is wrong there. I think children need to be exposed to all kinds of media, including television, but the content and mode or the way the programmes are built, whether it is advertising or a supposedly non-advertising category like 'News', should create a space for the children to learn. But increasingly, there is a homogenization, a dumbing down, and that prevents the child from developing his/her critical sensibility.

Mishra: Could you give us examples of inconsistencies and problems in selection of pieces for textbooks?

Bhattacharya: I can give you two different kinds of examples. One is when you create a textbook you have to look for variety. Then there are plenty of 'given' objectives, like introducing the child to her/his heritage and the past, creating links between the past and the present, and so on. Perhaps the government too puts forward its own agenda of creating an ideal citizen.

So my first response is to say that the textbook is a kind of impossible wish list. Everything that we ourselves are not and shall never be, we want the children to be. We want the choice of the lessons in the book, the literary pieces and the themes, everything, to reflect that ideal. We really should not proceed with this completely unrealistic map as it were, but look at clusters of issues and then choose texts that address these issues. In some cases, we don't really need to look for an issue, but may wish to select a poem or a story because it may provide us with a space to imagine in a powerful way, or because it uses language in a superb way, or because it bristles with interesting questions.

Of course, there has to be a degree of political awareness and responsibility towards the text. But I am saying you cannot merely choose a text because you have identified XYZ slots in advance and then you try to fill in the blanks. For example, the textbook writers have to represent 'the tribal'—in one instance, a piece by Verrier Elwin on 'Gonds' was chosen. There was an attempt here to fit the slot for the 'Other', the non-mainstream Indian. In this case, Elwin's piece itself is not bad, but the representation may not be appropriate for several reasons. One, because it is very dated. Second, the choice does not take into account the question of mediation, or how the writing of history has moved on. And finally, the exercises which follow the text enable only one kind of reading. Therefore, it is not only how you choose your 'literary piece', but how you frame and contextualize it, and finally what the child is expected to do with it that matters. Therein lies the real framework. For example, you can choose a wonderful poem by Tagore—which is in fact what they did in one of the West Bengal Primers. That poem (a *choda*) has so many local variations that it could be debated whether the poem is actually Tagore's or not. Anyway, Tagore gives it a certain version. However, when I visited schools I saw that the children were made to learn it by heart, quite mechanically, without any scope of enjoying the rhyme or the sounds or the words. Some children enjoyed the rhyme, the images, and were generally having fun with it, but that was despite the textbook and the teacher. Let me give you yet another example from Assam, of Bodo which is now officially a recognized state language, and there are new Bodo textbooks. One person I met had the job of writing the Bodo textbooks. What he did was to put in all his poems into the textbook and, frankly, they were quite bad—they were not really poems. But, quite apart from these 'non-poems' as it were, I heard from various other people many wonderful poems in Bodo, but they never found their way into the textbook, possibly because they were not considered 'literary' enough, whereas this gentleman was considered a published poet.

Your question is absolutely critical, and in response to it I can only tell you what should not be done; firstly, not to create a list and then seek to simply find representative texts, irrespective of caste, creed or colour. Somehow when you slot things you make them dead pieces. Secondly, one should not take a wonderful text and destroy it by 'textbooking' it. Because classroom transaction is a very different thing altogether; one has to be extremely attentive towards how to emphasize the text in the classroom, how it can come alive for and through the child. An equal amount of thought, planning, teacher training and everything else has to go into that process. And third (and the final) never fix the text and 'exercises' with finality. You have to constantly keep shifting things around, so in order to have ten texts you should have thirty alternative texts to play or work with.

Mishra: Do you mean that one should have a framework to develop a textbook as a finished product?

Bhattacharya: No, never as a 'finished' product! I see the texts in a textbook in a provisional form, with which the process of learning and teaching begins.

Mishra: What according to you should be the 'amounts' of fantasy and realism in children's literature?

Bhattacharya: Between what is called realism and fantasy, we see an in-between space, which is fluid and shifting. It is important of course, to ensure that the child is able to grapple with all those different stages of what is actually around him/her at any given point of time, and what makes life worth living or struggling for. And at the same time, also choose something that should enable the child to imagine something other than what exists in his/her everyday world. To me both these capacities are equally important. Besides there are fantastic moments in the everyday world.

Mishra: There is an ongoing debate to redefine the place of fantasy in school textbooks, and to strike a balance between fantasy and reality, with the latter being connected with 'value education'. Even if 'doses' of fantasy are checked at school, can they be checked at the level of family/home where stereotypes are perpetuated from fantasy and fairy tales, and does this not result in conflict/contradiction?

Bhattacharya: Can I complicate your question further? See, what is properly called 'value education' often ends up being didactic. It has a different face altogether. We assume that we—as teachers, writers, syllabus-makers—know what is 'value education', while you 'poor child' do not know anything; so let us tell you how life should be lived—that's the approach! Certainly, at one level children know less than we do. In some ways he or she is not in a position to scrutinize what we offer them. But, simply because he/she may be more uninhibited and less educated, children are actually in a position to be acutely aware of the gaps between what we preach and what we practise. It is most evident in the actual praxis of education, but is also present at home. Children learn very fast how to negotiate this gap—that what one learns and what one does—are two different things. Whether in school or at home this is what the child actually learns by his/her experience. Doing away with stereotypes at the representational level is useful, only upto a point.

Another aspect of value education is the exposure to 'reality'. In the West, for example, drug overdose, death by AIDS, pornography, child prostitution, divorce, etc. are seen as the problems of the real world that children will have to negotiate. It is believed that literature, particularly the one considered appropriate or necessary for teenagers, should address all these issues. Artists, at all times, have done this to a greater or lesser extent; but what I find new, is a conscious approach. It is not didacticism of the traditional kind. Nevertheless, it has a kind of value, or components of 'value education' in it, which may not always be the best thing for children's literature.

About fairytales and stereotypes: West Bengal had recently banned ghost stories and witches (as encouraging superstition) but fairy tales were allowed (as presumably being 'good' imagination). It is simply not a question of what to delete, erase or ban, but rather a question of how much do you respect the child? In what ways is a text of children's literature going to be mediated? Perhaps we do not pay enough attention to the fact that, whether it is written literature or visual, it does not happen in a vacuum—it always comes with a context. That is what I think is perhaps the most important thing for 'value education'. Children finally absorb what they experience as being of 'value'.

Mishra: Can you please tell us about 'Eurocentric' children's literature, and are there attempts to check it or Indianize it?

Bhattacharya: A huge question! It leads me to the example of Bangla literature, which is probably the 'richest' in terms of children's literature. I derive this opinion from others; they show a whole range of list of authors and books about children's literature to make this point. However, it can also be seen differently. In one of the *Yearly Reviews* (2004) brought out by the Department of English, we published the translation of an article by Sibaji Bandyopadhyay. He examines an entire corpus of adventure fiction in Bengali which comes out from the early twentieth century onwards. But it is totally Eurocentric in some of the basic subject positions, for example, the whole understanding and representation of Africa. So, if you say 'Bangla literature', then can I say their literature written in Bengali, by Bengali writers, addressing or concerned with a Bengali audience, and therefore, automatically, it is not Eurocentric? Clearly not.

Secondly, coming closer to the present, and based on my work with different publishers and groups producing literature for children, we find a very conscious attempt at producing bilingual texts, maybe in English or in any other Indian language, or have translations from these languages into English. It seems to me that while it is difficult to always identify Eurocentrism, what may be harder to do is to actually produce the 'Other'. Bringing out the folk tales in traditional/handmade paper is wonderful, but is it necessarily more 'authentic'/devoid of Eurocentrism? It is an open question. On the other hand, there are places within India where your next-door neighbour might appear more alien or exotic to you than an English or European person. I think there are attempts to negotiate this complexity in India and some signs are heartening, but it is not always done in a very conscious way. Another easy option seems to be to settle for something that seems obviously Indian (such as 'retelling' of the *Ramayana*) without even problematizing the process. To a great extent, we depend on actual interaction between what was earlier called 'vernacular' languages and English. And here too, it is more important to think in terms of how to negotiate the current configuration of market forces. 'Indianizing' will inevitably mean changing with the times, but in response to events around our everyday life, our political trajectories, things spoken and unspoken, thought of or not, memories, strands from the past, our desires for the future which is not closed—all this in the context of new forms of globalization.

7

For Learning to be Effective, the Student Has to Become a Maker of Meaning

Jonathan Gil Harris

Interviewed by Gitanjali Chawla and Prem Kumari Srivastava

Prem Kumari Srivastava: You have been in India for some time now and have had extensive interactions with varied student groups of universities in India. How has your experience been so far?

Jonathan Gil Harris: I have been visiting India for many years, but this is the first time I have lived here for an extended period. It's been an exhilarating 14 months. I've been a Visiting Fellow at Delhi University, Jawaharlal Nehru University, and Jadavpur University in Kolkata, and I've taught graduate classes in English Renaissance drama at each of them. I've also given talks at several undergraduate colleges in Delhi, as well as co-taught a course ('Shakespeare and the World') for the Young India Fellows Programme. During my time here, I've met an astonishing array of students from all over India. While many of them have come from relatively affluent Anglophone families, some are from much poorer, non-English-speaking backgrounds. Indeed, a number of students I have taught are not just the first members of their families to go to university; they are the first literate members of their families. It puts the

Earlier published in *FORTELL* Issue No. 26 (January 2013).

task of teaching English literature in stark perspective when I hear from my students that they've been busy teaching their parents how to read and write. While there are predictable infrastructure problems that have coloured my classroom experiences—not least power outages that have halted ceiling fans, raised temperatures, fogged brains, and turned me into a dripping mess—I have very much enjoyed working with the students here. After teaching for close to twenty-five years in New Zealand and the United States, I can now say that Indian students tend to differ in two crucial respects from their counterparts in the West, and in a way that might at first seem paradoxical. First, they are much more respectful of what they believe to be the professor's high status: I don't think I will ever get used to being called 'Sir', which to me seems like a relic from Tom Brown's school days. But, refreshingly, I have found that they are also much more inclined to argue with me—at least at the graduate level. Amartya Sen's *Argumentative Indian* is clearly alive and well in the ranks of India's MAs, MPhils and PhDs.

When I gave a lecture at JNU, the first comment in the Q and A period came from a student who said to me: 'Sir, I am deeply grateful to you for your informative and thoughtful presentation. But I must take deep and passionate issue with its theoretical premises.' His remark didn't feel hostile: it was born of a desire to engage with my argument. I have had many similar responses from my graduate students in the Young India Fellows Programme. It makes a welcome change from my experience in the comparatively conflict-averse US classroom, where vigorous disagreement, no matter how principled, is often regarded as a big no-no.

Gitanjali Chawla: While interacting with students in India, has there been a conscious or subconscious shift in your pedagogy?

Harris: Some of the shifts may have been subconscious, but at least one has been quite deliberate, and it is in direct response to the wide range in English language ability that I have encountered in the Indian classroom. When I taught a course at JNU, I was startled to find that even MA students in India's top graduate English programme struggled with the task of writing a conventional literary critical paper. Quite a few of them were not native speakers of English, and they had difficulty expressing themselves in a language made doubly foreign to them by the demand that they emulate the specialist jargon of academic English scholarship. I was shocked but not surprised, therefore, when a significant number of the students ended up plagiarizing all or part of their papers. This spate of plagiarism was also motivated, I suspect, by a saddening assumption: that there is one 'right' way of speaking about Shakespeare, that this 'right' way is completely disconnected from their own cultural and linguistic horizons, and that one must therefore copy the words of wise people in Britain and the US in order to speak with any authority about Shakespeare. I decided the problem was not really the students, who had been consistently terrific in class discussions, but rather the kind of writing assignments I was giving them. I needed to engage the students' specific abilities, and their local contexts, more effectively. And so I realized I needed to devise quite different writing assignments.

Chawla: Can you elaborate through examples of text(s) that you have taught in India?

Harris: When I next taught a graduate course, at the Young India Fellows Programme, I came up with a radically different syllabus. I taught a well-known work by Shakespeare, *The Tempest*, which I supplemented with creative re-imaginings of the play and its characters by playwrights, poets, filmmakers, and performance artists from around the world: the Caribbean playwright/politican Aimé Césaire's *A Tempest;* the US Cold War film *Forbidden Planet;* Suniti Namjoshi's lesbian-themed poems about Caliban and Miranda; Lemuel A. Johnson's African Caliban; the Mauritian Creole playwright Dev

Virahsawmy's *Toufann;* and Samoan choreographer Lemi Ponifasio's *Tempest Without A Body*. This syllabus impressed on the students that any interpretation of Shakespeare's play is not simply an attempt to arrive at the play's 'right' meaning (as if there were such a thing!). It is also a creative intervention that inevitably transforms the play from the vantage point of the interpreter's social, cultural and historical position. The final written assignment was designed to underscore the positionality of all interpretations. Instead of writing a conventional literary critical paper, each student produced a creative reimagining of *The Tempest* that drew on his/her own experiences. The result was stunning: I received profoundly thoughtful engagements with *The Tempest* that re-imagined it through the prisms of caste violence, honour killings, the myth of 'India Shining', Naxalite struggle, farmer suicides, etc. And best of all, the students came away from the course feeling they could read Shakespeare—not as passive recipients of his timeless wisdom, but as critical collaborators in the production of meaning.

Srivastava: Very often, students tend to just read a writer. How do you bring alive a writer like Shakespeare in the classroom? How do you transform a student, and I quote, 'from no idea about Shakespeare' to 'in love with Shakespeare'?

Harris: I'm not sure I can make anyone fall in love with Shakespeare—that's up to the student. But I can give my students basic tools with which to make sense of Shakespeare's English. For most Indian university students, even native speakers of English, Shakespeare's language can be intimidating in its foreignness. Not only are they daunted by his unfamiliar words, syntax, and rhetorical devices; they also tend to encounter Shakespeare exclusively on the page, where the machinery of scholarly editorial labour—rigid margins for prose passages, mysterious line breaks for verse passages, reams of explanatory footnotes and paratextual glosses—makes the task of reading particularly difficult, not to mention distracting. To read Shakespeare's plays as if they were novels, silently and in the privacy of one's own room, is usually a recipe for frustration and misunderstanding. Instead I stress to the students that Shakespeare's plays, even his lyric poems, were written to be heard. They should therefore be read out loud in company: indeed, the ear can hear meanings in the sounds of Shakespeare's language that the eye can't necessarily decipher from the page. Even in the US, where students are much more familiar with Shakespeare, they tend to be baffled by his language till they read it out loud. Here in India, I've found it particularly useful to get students together out of class to do a staged reading of any play they are about to study. That way, they can hear what Shakespeare's language is doing—and pause to make comments and ask questions. They may not understand everything about the play after reading it out loud with their classmates. But they certainly understand a lot more than they would have otherwise.

Srivastava: Do you think there is necessarily a need to align literature and language pedagogy? Many researchers are of the opinion that teachers of literature tend to lose sight of the fact that those teaching literature teach language as well and texts can be used to enhance language skills. How would you engage with the students in class keeping the above factor in mind?

Harris: On the one hand, to teach literature is to teach language. After all, literature is the artful use of language; it may also entail revolutionary ideas and powerful aesthetic experiences, but these are of necessity mediated by, and in language. I strongly believe that to read Shakespeare at all critically and effectively, one needs to have at least a basic grounding in prosody—it is important to know that the witches in *Macbeth*, for example, sound so eerie because Shakespeare has made them speak in an unusual rhythm (trochaic tetrameter) that deviates from the speech patterns of the other characters. Indeed, Shakespeare's supposed brilliance in creating vivid and memorable characters has a lot to do with his ability to deploy the acoustic properties of language in distinctive ways. And it is useful for a student to be able to account for his or her gut response to a character by being able to identify how exactly Shakespeare's language has in large part shaped that response. On the other hand, I don't believe that literature and language teaching should or can be fully collapsed into each other. Teaching the mechanics of literary English language—be it Shakespeare's dramatic verse or Jay-Z's hip-hop lyrics or Salman Rushdie's Hinglish prose—is an altogether different challenge from (say) teaching language to TOEFL/ESL students or teaching academic writing to engineering and business students. Each requires different skills. In the United States, English, Writing, and ESL departments are increasingly separate entities. And I think that's a welcome development. Professors of writing have usually been trained in rhetoric and composition, the arts of communication, persuasive argument, and so they are much better equipped to teach students across a range of disciplines how to write in various specialist forms of English. Similarly, professors of ESL are much better equipped to teach students about the grammatical rules and nuances of spoken and written English. I think this more capacious, multi-pronged model is one that Indian universities will adopt, and adapt, in the coming decade.

Chawla: Professor Harris, we have been peeping Toms and had a look at some of your students' comments on your Facebook page. The enthusiasm and excitement that you have generated is contagious and we are curious to know what exactly did you do in the classroom?

Harris: To be honest, I'm not sure I remember exactly what I did in the classroom. And that's because, even when I am lecturing to a large group of students, much of what happens in my classes is spontaneous and unscripted. For the classes I teach in India, I do prepare Power Point presentations that spell out some of my main points, accompanied by various images and passages from the set texts. (I've been suspicious of PPT in the past, but I've found it to be an effective tool in the Indian classroom where some of my students struggle to make sense of the language of the texts I'm teaching and even my accent.) But the Power Point presentation is more a supplement to, than the main event of the class. And that is because I expect the students to be active participants. To that end, I send them questions in advance of each class meeting, which I expect them to engage at length in the class discussion. I often make deliberately provocative, even outlandish, statements that are designed to get them thinking and talking. I also ask them to debate with each other. I strongly believe that real learning cannot happen in a classroom where students are simply passive recipients of what the teacher and the set text have to say. For the learning experience to be effective, the student has to become a maker of meaning too. Thinking out loud, playing with new ideas, engaging in the thought-experiment of 'what if this counterintuitive proposition were true'—all are important parts of what happens in my classroom.

Chawla: On the issue of showing slides of Shakespeare in boxers, as you have done, some conventional pedagogues might consider your approach trivial and extraneous. But the interest that you have elicited seems to belie this. How did you weave slides of Shakespeare in boxers into your pedagogy?

Harris: The instance to which you are alluding has a very specific context. The day before my last class in the Young Indian Fellows Programme, a student emailed me to say that as it was (apparently) International Boxers Day, she and her fellow students would all be coming to the next day's class wearing boxer shorts. I was tempted to wear a pair myself, but thankfully I desisted. Instead, I started my Power Point presentation the next day with an image of Shakespeare holding a skull—a la Hamlet with Yorick—all the while wearing boxer shorts. I followed it with a second slide, in which the same image was now accompanied by the caption:

'Hai, Yorick bechara. Main usko acchi tarah jaanta tha. Boxers mein'. ('Poor Yorick. I knew him very well. In boxers'.) Shakespeare does sound so much better in the original Hindi, don't you think? There's been a long tradition of treating Shakespeare's canon as a secular, literary version of scripture, to be treated with quasi-religious reverence and devotion. I had an English teacher at high school who would simply read out Shakespearean lines to us as if they were divine writ, and then he would stare at us imperiously till we nodded wisely and said things like 'brilliant!' or 'how true!' Of course, we never understood a word of what Shakespeare was actually saying. But by learning to nod, we had been successfully indoctrinated into that horrid cult that George Bernard Shaw so rightly called 'Bardolatry'. It is the epitome of anti-intellectualism, the kind of passive self-effacement that I seek to disable with my pedagogy. You don't love a distant God, you respect and fear him. To really love Shakespeare, one has to be able to talk with—and even back to—his texts. And that often means adopting a pose of strategic irreverence. When we're irreverent to Shakespeare, we are less likely to treat him as a God before whom we must fawn and more likely to regard him as a partner with whom we can do things—for instance, dress him in boxer shorts, but also creatively re-imagine his words in our modern-day contexts. When we are irreverent, we are more likely to take intellectual risks.

Srivastava: What are you currently working on?

Harris: I'm writing a book called *The First Firangis* which is based on a series of articles I wrote for *The Hindustan Times* last year. It's about nine migrants from Europe, Africa and Asia who settled in India before the age of British colonialism. Despite being foreigners, these migrants became desi in ways that had a profound impact on what we now consider indigenous Indian culture. Amber Malik, a slave from Ethiopia, served as the regent of the Nizamshah dynasty of Ahmadnagar and founded the city that was to become Aurangabad. Thomas

Stevens, a dissident Catholic priest from England, wrote one of the classic Marathi Puranas. Augustin Hiriart Hunarmand, a jeweller from the Basque region of France, served in Jahangir's and Shah Jahan's courts and probably designed the legendary peacock throne of the Mughals. Dara Shikoh's spiritual advisor Sa'id Sarmad died revered as a Sufi saint and a Hindu yogi, but he was born as a Jew in Armenia. These four people, and the other men and women I examine in *The First Firangis* complicate what it means to be 'authentically' Indian—and reveal the extraordinary cosmopolitanism of the subcontinent's pre-colonial history. Like the nine migrants of my book, I am a foreigner, but I also am not: my time in India has transformed me, changing how I speak, how I think, what I wear, what I eat, the music I listen to. Slowly but surely, like the word firangi itself 'main Hindustani ban raha hoon' ('I am becoming a Hinustani'). This book is an extended meditation on that process of becoming as it has unfolded for me, and as it unfolded for nine others at a time when the violence of three centuries of British colonialism was yet to happen. It's impossible to disavow that later history. But we also need to think against and beyond it in order to imagine alternative, unexpected forms of cross-cultural contact. And in the process, we might begin to recognize that what we think of as authentically Indian has so often been the product of transnational migrations and mixings.

8

Need to Focus on the Process of Writing

Jackie-Lynn Van Tilburgh

Interviewed by Mukti Sanyal

Mukti Sanyal: What is the English Language Fellow Program? Why did you want to participate in it?

Jackie-Lynn Van Tilburgh: The EL Fellow Program is a collaboration of the US State Department and Georgetown University. Its goal is to send TESOL educators around the globe to work with students, teachers, and teacher educators to improve English instruction and promote better cross-cultural understanding.

I joined it because I thought it would be a great opportunity to teach overseas and visit a new country. I've travelled extensively and have been teaching for over fifteen years, but I'd never taught overseas, and I'd never been to India prior to my placement here. It's been a fascinating opportunity, and I think I've learned much more than I've taught.

Sanyal: How can other Indian schools and universities get involved with the EL Fellow Program?

Tilburgh: If a particular school or college would like to work with an EL Fellow, the Principal at the institution should submit a formal request, outlining a specific plan for the work that he or she would like the Fellow to achieve to the RELO office in New Delhi.

Earlier published in *FORTELL* Issue No. 31 (July 2015).

Sanyal: What has been your impression of how we teach English in Indian colleges and universities? What do you make of the divide between language and literature in the teaching of English in Indian academic circles? What has been your experience?

Tilburgh: I think that it is a shame that there can't be a place for both language and literature. There is definitely more value placed on the study of literature, while language study is seen as a more remedial endeavour. The discussion and analysis of literature provides a basis for critical thinking, which is an important lifelong skill, no matter what the future occupation. However, with less than 25 per cent of the Indian population speaking English and with various degrees of proficiency, I think there is a real need for an increase in language courses. While most will never need to discuss the major themes in *Pride and Prejudice*, the vast majority could benefit from basic communicative English language practice. Whether we like it or not, English is the language of twenty-first century commerce, and if Indian students want to compete in the globalized marketplace, they need to be proficient in speaking English. If literature classes were to be more discussion-based, both critical thinking and communicative language needs could be met simultaneously, bridging the language/literature divide.

Sanyal: Why is it that, in spite of our best efforts, we are not able to get our students to speak, as opposed to read and write?

Tilburgh: People, in general, like to do what's familiar; they don't like to be out of their comfort zone. Reading and writing are the skills that are practised most often in Indian schools, so it is difficult to change this pattern in an eighteen-year-old college student who has grown up in such a system.

Additionally, reading and writing allow for more time for self-correction. If verbal errors are made, however, everyone knows it immediately. Students like reading and writing more because their mistakes are not as public. While no one likes to make mistakes, I've noticed that Indian students are particularly hesitant to take the risks necessary to improve their spoken English communication. Teachers, unwittingly, can contribute to this lack of confidence by over-emphasizing form over meaning. For example, during a recent conversation that I was having with a student, her professor interrupted her mid-sentence to point out grammatical errors. This interruption made the student more self-conscious and encouraged her to speak less, not more. As teachers, I believe that we need to focus on building confidence first and foremost.

Another obstacle is that teachers are more comfortable with reading and writing practice. They may not have strong skills, and listening and speaking activities expose their own vulnerabilities. Thus, they emphasize reading and writing tasks and perpetuate this cycle.

Sanyal: Is it to do with the situation in India, of having a common L1 that students can comfortably fall back on, as opposed to the US, in a class of 45, there might be several different L1s?

Tilburgh: While a common L1 and class size do indeed contribute to the problem, in my opinion, the biggest obstacle is the classroom design: rows of difficult-to-move desks, windows open to loud street traffic, and noisy fans. All these contribute to making conversation and discussion extremely difficult. In my classes here, I've had to rearrange desks daily, shout to be heard over fans and street traffic, and constantly ask students to repeat their responses in louder voices. This makes a teacher's already tiring job exhausting. But I've also found that once students get into the habit, they will automatically group desks, and, tiring of having to repeat themselves, they will begin speaking louder. It can be done.

Sanyal: How can EL Fellows gain more from their exchange? How could we structure our hosting situations to better the Fellow experience?

Tilburgh: The EL Fellow Program schedule (late August to late June) is a poor fit with the Indian academic calendar. Since Fellows are already starting well into the first semester, it would be best to have as much pre-planning done before their arrival. Having a concrete class schedule and definitive list of student participants would be ideal. In addition, it would be extremely advantageous to give some sort of time compensation (fewer classes, etc.) to the host institution's primary point of contact. This person has a lot to coordinate, so adequate preparation time is needed to ensure that the host institution is fully benefitting from the Fellow's presence.

Sanyal: What has your work been like here?

Tilburgh: I've been really fortunate in that I've had the opportunity to work here in Bharati College (University of Delhi), as well as in a government university, and for a non-profit organization. Each experience has been unique. Here at Bharati College, my focus has been on teaching eight-week intensive courses on academic reading and writing. I've got to know my students well and have seen their progress over time. While Indian students do a lot of writing, the focus tends not to be on the *process* of writing. My experience has been that students write an assignment the day before it is due, without any thought to an essay's organization and without time for revision. When students are forced to spend the time making outlines, revising drafts, and editing their work, they are quite pleased with their final products and see the advantage of spending more time with their writing. It's exciting to see them put their newly-learned skills into practice and develop more confidence as writers.

In my other university assignment, I conduct writing workshops for larger groups and meet individual students to discuss their writing. While the large numbers and less frequent meetings have not allowed me the opportunity to get to know students on the same level as here at Bharati College, I have enjoyed the greater diversity of a co-educational campus with both undergraduate and postgraduate students. I have seen that students, no matter what the level, really crave one-on-one attention to help them improve their writing skills. It's really a shame that large class sizes make this type of interaction difficult here.

Although my time has been spent primarily with academic reading and writing, my NGO work has allowed me to focus on creating communicative activities to help young girls from underprivileged backgrounds gain more confidence in their speaking abilities. I have enjoyed this less-academic fun pursuit, and it has been a delight to meet these very motivated young ladies.

Sanyal: Which group of learners do you find most satisfying?

Tilburgh: Isn't that a bit like asking a parent who her favourite child is? I really love all my students. However, if you really twist my arm, I would have to say that I particularly enjoyed the two-week language workshop that I just finished with a group of *mumukshus*, Jain nuns-in-training in Rajasthan. They truly loved to be in the classroom and had a real eagerness to learn; their zeal was infectious. I really appreciated their inquisitiveness and playfulness. It may be that it's the most recent experience that I've had, so it's fresher in my mind. It may also have to do with the fact that I had the opportunity to team-teach with another Fellow there. I always find it exciting to work with other innovative teachers.

Sanyal: The time you spent with the library staff at Bharati College has been much appreciated, and your workshop with the non-teaching staff was a big hit. Would you like to talk about that? I don't mind confessing that though I have helped organize several workshops for English teachers from other institutions, we have never attempted anything for our own non-teaching/adminstrative staff.

Tilburgh: I love working with classes of non-traditional students. The non-teaching staff workshop was so much fun! Those who have been out of the classroom for some time do not take a minute of learning time for granted. They showed such appreciation during our week together, and their participation was fantastic. They really took the opportunity seriously, and I think they made considerable progress in their English skills in just that brief week. It would be great if it could be made a part of their regular professional development.

Sanyal: All of us at Bharati College will miss you, Jackie! It's wonderful to see how friendly you have been. I'm looking forward to the workshops you will be running for teachers in early May. Can you please talk briefly about that?

Tilburgh: In order to have an impact beyond the ten months that I am here, the Principal, Dr. Promodini Varma has requested that I train other English teachers in conducting intensive reading and writing courses of their own next year. I'm hoping to have interactive sessions where I show teachers what I did this past year, and we brainstorm ways to tailor it to fit their own teaching styles.

Sanyal: How do your teaching duties here differ from your duties in the US?

Tilburgh: I think that there are more possibilities for collaboration in the US. I work extensively with my colleagues there to design engaging lessons, brainstorm solutions to dealing with difficult students, and create cross-curricular courses. We have the luxury of office space, and use it to our advantage—lots of coffee-fuelled discussion! In addition, my class sizes are smaller in the US, so I am able to meet individual students more often. During a semester, I may have individual writing conferences with students three or four times during the semester. Here, I was only able to have two conferences per semester.

Also, the idea of office hours is much more common in the US. I have set periods of time every day when I am in my office, with the sole purpose of meeting students to address questions and doubts. Here, although I set aside time, only a handful of students come to see me. I have to work hard to convince them that they aren't bothering me; I really do want them to come to me with their questions.

Sanyal: What impact do you hope to have here?

Tilburgh: I'm not naïve enough to think that I can make huge changes in a ten-month time span. However, I do hope that my students have more confidence in their skills after our time together. In addition, many of the students that I've taught here want to be future teachers. If I have in any way helped to show them that fun and learning are not mutually exclusive ideas, and they become teachers who make their own classrooms spaces of creative student engagement, then my time here will have been spent productively.

9

The Real Goal is to Improve Proficiency

Dee Broughton

Interviewed by Iqbal Judge

Iqbal Judge: As part of your work as Senior Language Fellow in India, what is your assessment of the language teaching scenario?

Dee Broughton: Well, I'm constantly impressed by how interested teachers are in doing good things with their students, despite the obstacles and challenges they have to contend with. In India, there is a great deal of emphasis on assessment, and we see a lot of effect that has on the teaching and on the learning and not all of it is very effective. Teachers are expressing the desire to change the assessment so that the teaching can change, so that the entire system can produce more English language users, with a greater ability to use the language skilfully in different situations. I feel they need a change of emphasis in assessment from literature to proficiency, so that they can move from teaching literature to English proficiency.

Judge: You place great emphasis on teaching academic writing to students. Why?

Broughton: From what I've seen, there is no real teaching of academic writing in India, in fact I haven't seen any. It doesn't mean that it doesn't exist, but it certainly isn't widespread. I see people who are admitted into MPhil programmes, and

Earlier published in *FORTELL* Issue No. 27 (July 2013).

that's the first time they do extended writing. From my point of view that's quite late and so I would love to see more writing at school level. My emphasis right now is on training teachers to introduce academic writing at the undergraduate level, so that by the time people get to MPhil or PhD programme, they have actually quite a lot of basic experience in using sources, structuring complex ideas, etc. and are equipped to do real research. My strong belief is that academic writing is the way to share ideas and solve problems in the world, and we need the ideas and researches of Indian scholars to be included in that; and in order to do that they need to publish internationally. So we need to raise particularly their ability to use sources, to cite properly, and to connect those to their own ideas. My focus is on the use of sources and on the structures that academic writing uses to organize ideas. Smaller issues like grammar, etc. can be fixed after the ideas are expressed clearly and shared properly.

Judge: Isn't this a kind of paradigm shift then, for us teachers in India, because here the focus seems to be on teaching literature and improving grammar?

Broughton: Exactly! I think it's definitely a paradigm shift because in the past focusing on literature has also led to focus on 'the facts of the text'. Sometimes literature is not even taught in English at all; it's taught in a class in a native language like Hindi or Gujarati, and it's a 'cultural approach' to literature, we're teaching about literature, and not actually teaching the text. So, yes, this is a huge shift, because to build proficiency in a language you need to focus on the language, and often people do think it means focusing on grammar or whatever, but it doesn't mean just that. Even more importantly, if you focus on writing, there's a focus on things like: Look carefully at this text to see how the writer did this ...why did the writer use all these adjectives... why did the writer punctuate it this way... why did they use dialogue here ... what changes in the meaning of a text when the writer does this or that? That is what focusing on the language means.

Teachers need to be constantly reminded that the real goal is to improve proficiency, it's not to produce a perfect paragraph about a particular poem or story, it's to produce a student body that is capable of writing a paragraph about anything, that will make sense to other people—and that's very different. Because in one case you may be trying to model a paragraph for your students to repeat it perfectly and in another you'll teach them to think deeply about what they read, and to respond with ideas and how to organize those in ways that other people will understand.

Judge: This would mean then, that the students must actively engage with the text; but very often one finds that some students—particularly those used to the 'teacher explains in the mother-tongue and students memorise method' can't understand the text at all, or at least most parts of it.

Broughton: See, there is the idea of comprehensible input. It's very important at low levels of learning English that students be given information that they can understand in the language. You have to understand about 85 per cent of what you read, in order to learn the other 15 per cent that you don't understand. So if we want students to learn new things from language, then it has to be mostly comprehensible in the beginning. One of the things we have been working on is the idea of what makes it comprehensible, considering their vocabulary.

Judge: In the workshop you conducted on 'Teaching Academic Writing', you mentioned some internet sites that teachers could use to check whether a particular text would be comprehensible for a particular level of students.

Broughton: There are a few sites that I use a lot. You can look up Paul Nation; he's a big name in vocabulary, a very generous researcher, he distributes many of his findings, data, and the tests he has devised. There's also a software he's devised, called 'Range'. You can feed a text part into it and it will give you a report that tells you how many of the words in that text fall into the most common list of words, and how many into the next most common and how many are in the academic list, so it gives teachers or textbook writers an awareness of how common the vocabulary is in that piece.

Judge: You have also laid great emphasis on stimulating thinking.

Broughton: Yes, that's the second keystone of my approach to building language proficiency. People acquire language only by using language meaningfully. And you can only use language meaningfully if you are thinking. In order to organize your thoughts, you have to have thoughts; in order to use language, you have to have something to say. So we need to stimulate thinking, to encourage students to think about the input, to think about the story, letter, text or whatever, in ways that will help them to produce more language. Therefore, we need more open-ended questions, less of yes-no questions, or questions that already suggest an answer. And then, one of the ways in which people show they've learnt the language, especially in an academic or testing situation, is to write. Most of the time proficiency is also being tested through writing. The other is simply that writing is thinking. We, as a human species, can't have very complex thoughts without writing, because we can't hold all of them down in our heads at one time. We have to write things in order to remember them, we have to analyze them, and revise our thoughts to make them clear. All that requires writing. So writing is thinking.

Judge: What about encouraging spoken interaction, doing brainstorming, etc.?

Broughton: I suppose you can do some of that in speaking, but programmes that start by teaching speaking only bring your student up to a certain level; yes, you can get a job, you know, in some service fields with good spoken English, but that is not going to raise the level of India in international academic standards. People don't have high-level ideas about research orally; you write them down. So that's why we focus on writing.

Judge: Could you give us a glimpse, perhaps by way of an example, of how, even at lower levels, teachers could bring students to engage in higher order thinking, and how to structure an academic discourse?

Broughton: Well, the important thing is to get your students to think about and engage with real problems, real issues in their lives, and to write about them. Something that isn't in the story or the text that they've read, but is possible in real life. For example, if it's an article or story about inventions, children could be asked to think of and list inventions that they think are important. Then, each student would be asked to think about what makes these inventions 'important'. Does 'important' mean that something is popular? Does it mean that it saves lives or helps people? Is something more important if it helps more people? Each student would need to think about their definition of 'important'. The text must actually serve as a spring board to spark off thinking and this exercise helps to develop logic and evaluation skills. Children should be stimulated with open questions to realize that the idea of 'importance' is relative. There is no 'right' answer to what makes something important, but it is important to critical thinking to realize that when people say something is important, they have some criteria in mind for what that means. I mentioned earlier about citing sources, and the structures that academic writing uses to organize ideas. These too can be dove-tailed into the above activity. For example, each student would need to ask at least six, or eight, or ten others, what they thought an important invention was, and why, or what their definition of 'important' was. They would then need to present their findings in writing, using the structures that the teacher would have already given them, 'Some people think that', 'Others say', etc.

Judge: That sounds interesting and doable. It would engage the students, makes them use language, ask questions, note down responses, categorize the responses, become aware of different viewpoints, and also give them the 'content' for writing.

Broughton: Yes, and you can see that this simple organizational format can be used at different levels, from the simplest to more advanced, complex pieces of academic writing—research papers, for instance.

10

English as Lingua Franca Will Embrace a Range of Usages

Penny Ur

Interviewed by Tara Chadha

Tara Chadha: I understand that you decided to migrate from your native country some three decades ago. What inspired you to make Israel your permanent home?

Penny Ur: I was going to study Hebrew and Arabic at Oxford, so in my 'gap year' I decided to go to Israel and learn modern Hebrew. I stayed on a kibbutz on an 'Ulpan' scheme which allows you to work half the day and study half the day for five months, and acquired a basic knowledge of modern Hebrew that way. But I also fell in love with the kibbutz idea and the country, and decided I would make it my home. I returned to the UK to finish my degree and teaching diploma, and then emigrated to Israel.

Chadha: You have been a practising teacher and a teacher trainer. How far has your experience as a school teacher helped you to carve out the agenda of your training programmes and teaching materials?

Ur: I have been for most of my working life a practising teacher of English; my writing and teacher training grew out of this. To this day, I see myself primarily as a teacher (it's what I automatically write when I have to mention my 'occupation').

Earlier published in *FORTELL* Issue No. 18 (May 2010),

I have since researched, published and lectured as part of my work as an academic; but my thinking is shaped primarily by my own professional classroom experience.

Chadha: What basic difference do you find between dealing with young school children and mature users of English language?

Ur: Young and older learners respond in different ways. Adult learners are more cognitively and metacognitively developed, can make use of more abstract explanations (grammar rules, for example), or of conscious, effective learning strategies—and use them to inform their own developing proficiency. Young learners learn more intuitively, so it is better to use activities that have them learning by heart or playing games or by listening to stories, that is acquiring the language through meaningful rehearsal and exposure. In a classroom environment, incidentally, older learners learn much faster than younger ones, so that's another difference.

Chadha: In the situation of learning English as a second or third language (as in India) which of the skills should be given priority?

Ur: This one is very difficult to answer! It depends on what the learners need English for. If it's for work in call centres, then obviously listening and speaking skills should be preferred. If it's for advancement in an academic career, then perhaps reading and writing. Internationally, perhaps, because of the development of IT, the skills of reading and writing are becoming more important than they were previously, and for many learners will take priority.

Chadha: Earlier the emphasis was on reading and writing but with globalization and focus on communicative methods, the emphasis has shifted to the oral skills. In our situation teachers and resource persons are not well exposed to listening and speaking. Even when they have mastery of grammar and lexis of the language, they cannot speak with confidence and fluency. As a teacher trainer could you suggest some methods and materials for a situation like ours to help the teachers?

Ur: I'm not sure I agree with your first statement, as I said above, the development of IT internationally has meant the development of the use of the written skills: for emails, 'chat', SMS, Twitter, Facebook and so on, which taken together have to a large extent supplanted the telephone as the major channel of communication. Having said that, I would agree that the oral skills are primary and essential, and how to develop confidence and fluency in the use of the oral language is a huge challenge. There are some books which suggest ideas for speaking activities, for example my book *Discussions That Work* and Frederike Klippel's *Keep Talking*. But it's also important that coursebooks dealing with general courses in English should have components that provide the students with opportunities to use speaking skills and develop their fluency.

Chadha: How much importance should be given to the teaching of grammar at different levels?

Ur: I think grammar is fairly important, and that there should be an explicit grammar syllabus of the basic structures at elementary and secondary school level, with the grammar structures being taught and prastised systematically. At the tertiary level probably grammar will be taught rather 'reactively', i.e. the teacher will respond to lack of knowledge or mistakes as she encounters them, and take time occasionally to draw students' attention to correct usage.

The methods change as students get older: younger students benefit from a lot of learning by heart, game-like practice, and simple, concrete, explanations. Older students, with more highly developed cognitive and metacognitive abilities can cope with more generalized and abstract explanations, and more demanding practice. At school level, I would estimate that grammar teaching in any case should not take up more than about half a lesson a week on an average: the rest of the time should be devoted to teaching vocabulary and the four skills.

Chadha: You have been interacting with a cross section of users of English in India. How would you place them vis-à-vis the users of English in other countries?

Ur: The people I've been meeting and talking to have been people with MA or even PhD degrees in English literature, so I wouldn't claim to have met a cross section. These people have excellent knowledge of English which is comparable to academics in other countries I've visited.

Chadha: During the course of your workshop on material development, you made an observation that the majority of English speakers today are located, to use Kachru's terms, in the 'outer' or 'expanding circles', using English as a lingua franca. Do the native speakers of English consider this global linguistic development as some sort of threat to the monopoly they have enjoyed for years or do they feel happy that English has acquired a global status?

Ur: I think on the whole native English speakers are quite happy that English has achieved the status of a lingua franca: those of them who speak a fairly 'standard' variety of English are thereby enabled to communicate with all sorts of people worldwide with whom they could not communicate before. Those who speak a 'non-standard' variety—like 'Singlish' for example, or Afro-American English—need to develop the ability to function in Standard English side by side with their 'native' dialect.

Chadha: In what way is English as a lingua franca different from the Standard English variety? Could you spell out some of its linguistic features? Has this variety been codified to be used as a teaching-learning model in a second language learning situation like that of India? If it has not been codified, who will be the deciding authority in the event of any dispute?

Ur: Users of English as a lingua franca have to use some kind of Standard English, defined as that variety (or range of varieties) of English that will be universally comprehensible and acceptable worldwide. This is very similar to, for example,

American English, or Indian English; the only difference is that speakers of these varieties need to 'weed out' those items which are peculiar to their native community and not used worldwide: *fortnight* in British English, for example, or *lakh* in Indian English.

No, there is no codification at present. I think there is likely to be some kind of 'wiki' that will provide the information necessary, contributed to by linguists from all over the world. I doubt if there will be any 'authority' that will decide on which is preferable. It is likely that the speakers of the language will decide, gradually one usage will become predominant. The experience of academics, as in France, who try to proclaim what shall be the 'right' way to say things is that this kind of authoritative imposition doesn't work: it's the speakers of the language on the street who eventually decide. It will be the same, surely, with ELF.

Chadha: Despite the fact that local varieties of English have cropped up and are widely used in different parts of the world. There is a strong bias against the local varieties, do you see any possibility of a similar bias against FLF?

Ur: As I said in my talk, there is an interesting phenomenon of the growth and flourishing of different 'Englishes' at the same time as the growth of ELF. I don't think there's any contradiction. And I don't really understand or sympathize with the bias against local varieties as 'inferior'; they have the same right to exist and be respected as any other language or dialect. I doubt if the same problem will arise with ELF; it isn't a variety linked to any particular (superior or inferior) community, but rather an instrument, a useful tool, for achieving certain communicative goals.

Chadha: What, in your opinion, has led to the rise of ELF?

Ur: We need to divide this question into two: why a worldwide lingua franca, and why English? There is a need for a worldwide lingua franca simply because of the rapid increase in contact between people around the world due to the amazing developments in communications technology and increased speed and amount of international travel. At the same time, various fields of human activity (business, entertainment, finance, politics, scientific research and so on) are rarely limited to one country these days; if they are international, they need to have a common language in which to function.

As to why English, mainly because at the same time as all these developments were occurring and the need for a lingua franca arose, English happened to be the most widely spoken language already in the world. The reasons for the spread of English were mainly political, military or economic: the expansion of the British Empire in the nineteenth century, and the economic and political power of the United States in the twentieth century, to give two examples. It has nothing to do with the linguistic characteristics of English itself.

Chadha: What relationship do you visualize between ELF and the Standard English variety? Do you think that ELF will be able to acquire a sort of complete autonomy?

Ur: I think ELF will be a 'standard' variety of English, in the sense of being universally comprehensible but this standard variety is likely to embrace a range of usages, not just one 'correct' usage—as indeed does any language. So no, I don't think it will ever be a separate, uniformly accepted autonomous language with only one set of 'correct' form in terms of its grammar, vocabulary and pronunciation. As long as its usages are universally comprehensible, it will tolerate a variety of forms and different accents.

Professional Development of Teachers

11

Teachers' Growth Arises from the Process of Reflecting on Classroom Experiences

N.S. Prabhu

Interviewed by Nupur Samuel

Nupur Samuel: You have made some insightful observations about teachers' professional development in your article 'Teachers' Growth'. Please tell us how teachers can grow professionally through everyday activities and what are some of the practical ways which may help teachers to become empowered for their professional growth?

N.S. Prabhu: I believe teachers' growth arises from ongoing teaching activities—the process of thinking about and making sense of one's classroom experiences, reflecting on those and using them to improve one's teaching. The paper 'Teachers' Growth' describes the types of activity likely to support/enhance that process. That paper, however, is only speculative, in the sense that it states some possibilities which need to be tried out and reviewed, probably throwing up in the process other possibilities. The occurrence of this latter—teachers thinking of new possibilities in the course of acting on existing ones—is for me a form of empowerment.

Samuel: Could you elaborate on some activities that are likely to prompt teachers to reflect and consequently engage with

Earlier published in *FORTELL* Issue No. 25 (September 2012).

various possibilities?

Prabhu: There are four activities that can prompt such a process. Observing a class in progress, whether one's own (video recorded) or a colleague's at any level. Here I do not mean observing the class for identifying or categorizing anything but simply to see what is happening. I believe there is something about viewing a lesson in progress that touches a teacher more than any talking about teaching can. Teachers thinking about and making sense of their classroom experience, has for me the most central, most essential role, and I am asking how we can make teachers become critical thinkers, who do not passively accept what others ask them to think or how others expect them to act. I am arguing for a more active, engaging role by teachers for their own professional development that can be strengthened and supported by others (trainers, specialists).

The second activity is the teacher exercising his/her own judgement in making decisions about what to teach or what activity to conduct with particular classes/in particular lessons. These decisions could be guided by memories of how things had gone in past lessons or by a teacher's experience about the class at that point or simply by a wish to find out by experiment. The more decisions the teacher makes, the more stake he/she has in how the lesson goes and therefore the stronger reason to look back and interpret/assess the lesson afterwards. It may not be possible to do this with each lesson but even irregular, occasional use of it is likely to add to pedagogic judgment and professional growth.

The third activity that I would like to talk about is attempting to communicate one's current pedagogic understanding to a colleague. This can be challenging, since one's own understanding is still not fully developed, is uncertain and less than accessible. However, the very act of trying to articulate a half-formed, vague idea, perception or understanding, helps to make it more intelligible and more accessible to oneself. A teacher's attempt to articulate his/

her pedagogic understanding at a given point in time can be useful in clarifying one's understanding and furthering it. An added benefit is the possibility of conveying it to a colleague and thus building a shared knowledge system.

An extension of this idea is to interact with specialists and this is the fourth activity that I want to suggest. Of course, this is more challenging than sharing one's ideas with a colleague but it is a valuable source of teachers' growth. Usually, teachers' perceptions and ideas are in a formative, uncertain stage; more importantly, they are also necessarily, personal and subjective. Though specialists' arguments too are very often based on their own pedagogic perceptions, they are moulded to fit the conventions of academic discourse and stated as part of some more general, objective truth. When teachers have developed some confidence in their own perceptions, they can perhaps penetrate the professional convention and deal with academic discourse with greater confidence, thus making contact with specialists' perceptions.

Samuel: In your interview with Alan Maley in *The Teacher Trainer* (1989), you mentioned that you would like to adopt the 'process writing' approach to help teachers clarify their ideas, develop thoughts and help reflective practices. Have you had some success in this? If yes, please tell us about it.

Prabhu: What I have in mind is the process of trying to state in words precisely what one has in mind. This can be a trying, frustrating process which does not lead to a quick or satisfying product, but it is so because it constantly throws up various other possibilities of wording—and some of these other wordings lead one to look back at what one had in mind. That produces fresh interpretations of one's own thought, which in turn needs a fresh attempt at wording. The experience in general multiplies one's interpretations and leads one towards a deeper and more differentiated understanding. I see this as the most valuable lesson of the 'process writing' movement. I have tried to put this view of mine to students in Singapore (secondary school teachers upgrading their qualifications) and to get them to observe themselves while trying to write their assignments, but can only say that the try-out has increased my own confidence in the view. A one-semester course—about ten weekly encounters of two hours each—is not long enough for more visible evidence.

Samuel: As you had mentioned in your article 'Hoping for the Best' (1999), learning is accidental, it is individual, even private. Since the process of learning is unpredictable and intangible, how can teachers understand it to improve their instructions and teaching?

Prabhu: The process of learning (as a mental phenomenon) is invisible, but not the product of it. When something has been learnt, that fact is revealed fairly clearly by the learner's subsequent performance. The teacher can easily be guided by whether there is evidence of something having been learnt, in contrast to earlier evidence to the contrary.

Although we cannot predict which of the things we teach will be learnt, we can predict that some of the things taught over a time will be learnt; and we can also see whether more has been learnt in one case than in another. This enables us to prefer one kind of lesson plan, classroom procedure or activity over another, and thus to arrive at more and more effective teaching procedures.

Samuel: India today is faced with the massive task of teacher training across the country. Could you suggest some methods for large-scale implementation of newer ideas in language pedagogy?

Prabhu: I am disillusioned with large-scale implementation of new ideas in language pedagogy—not just with past attempts at it but with the concept itself. I doubt that good teaching results from new ideas, unless they are the teachers' own (evolving) ideas, and believe that individual teachers have the potential to develop ideas. The number of teachers overall has little effect on the growth potential of individual teachers.

Samuel: In your articles you write that you believe that trying out ideas and interacting with people, getting their response, etc, leads to professional growth of teachers. Do you place any importance to teachers' disagreement with the prevailing or dominant view in their professional growth? What can teachers do to hold meaningful dialogues with researchers and specialists, given the fact that differences exist?

Prabhu: Yes, I do believe that disagreement is generally more productive for new thought than its opposite, and the search for a better way to teach begins with a belief that the current way is not the best. I wouldn't, however, specially want to disagree with something because it is prevalent or dominant. I think it is more important not to hold back from disagreeing with things that are at variance with our current understanding, whether those things are other people's views or our own past views. This is because stopping to disagree with things is stopping to (re-)think about them—and stopping to grow. An ultimate teaching method with which we can all live in satisfaction can only be a convenient myth.

References

Maley, A. (1989). Interview with N.S. Prabhu. *Teacher Trainer Journal* 3/3. http://www.tttjournal.co.uk/uploads/File/back_articles/Interview_with_ Dr_Prabhu.pdf

Prabhu, N.S. (2004). 'Teachers' Growth'. Melaka Conference, May 2004.

Prabhu, N.S. (1999). Teaching is at most hoping for the best. (RELC Conference) Singapore, 1998. In Christopher Ward and Willy Renandya, eds. *New Insights for the Language Teacher*. Singapore: RELC.

12

Teachers Should Not be Obsessed with Outcomes

Rod Bolitho

Interviewed by Prem Kumari Srivastava and Sabina Pillai

Prem Kumari Srivastava: It is has been a pleasure interacting with you for the whole day in this intensive workshop on 'Classroom Observation and Supervision' organized by Professor Rama Mathew, Coordinator Minds Project (Mentoring in Delhi Schools) in collaboration with the British Council, New Delhi.

Rod Bolitho: I hope everybody enjoyed the workshop as much as I did.

Sabina Pillai: Yes, we did. What brings you to India this time?

Bolitho: I have been involved in a Policy Debate on the future of ELT in India. The British Council has organized a Think Tank on it and I am here for its second meeting on Continual Professional Development (CPD).

Pillai: CPD is not yet a widely recognized or acknowledged concept in India. How do you view it in the Think Tank?

Bolitho: CPD is not exclusive to the teaching profession. The interest in it stems from a wider context. For example, it has been prevalent in the engineering, medical and other professional fields where people were keen to know what

---

Earlier published in *FORTELL* Issue No. 22 (September 2011).

others were doing in their respective fields. Part of the mandate of the Think Tank is to raise awareness about it amongst principals and education managers. CPD need not just be in-service training. Any professional development activity for that matter can be seen as CPD.

There is a direct link between the individual and the institution here. An institution's development depends on its staff's professional development. It is a good indicator of the professional climate in an institution.

Pillai: When will we hear about the recommendations of the Think Tank? Is there any schedule for the roll out of this programme?

Bolitho: I am sure that there will be a strategic launch of the programme, supported by a publication in due course. I am not sure when that will happen.

Srivastava: You have been associated with the CBSE Curriculum Report project in India since 1989. It is 2011 today. What are your observations on the Indian education system and particularly the way English teaching is being handled? Have you noticed some significant changes?

Bolitho: I think there is a marked shift in the way English is perceived in India today. David Graddol's book *English Next*, now available online, established that English is very much a tool for economic growth in the country. I remember a time when it was seen as a postcolonial legacy and therefore faced a lot of hostility. It was percieved as an alien force. That is no longer the case. This shift is also felt in the CBSE school curricula. In fact Indian English has come of age. I rememeber the time when Indians used 'only' in every sentence. There are recognizable varieties of Indian English today. Then, there was a generous use of the present progressive forms. Interestingly, even today these archaic usages are found in India. What immediately comes to my mind is the all too familiar: I want 'to nab' or 'lakhs and crores'. Beyond the subcontinent, I doubt if anybody can understand these expressions.

Srivastava: Looking at your vast repertoire of scholarship, it is clear that you have been keenly interested in understanding the negotiation of classroom pedagogy of English language. What interests you the most?

Bolitho: I have been in Teacher Education and Training for over 30 years. Initially I was in Teacher Training and also got involved in in-service training. Then I saw the wider implications. Interestingly, I came down to India with Adrian Underhill to meet and write about the self-help group called English Language Teaching Community (ELTC) in Bangalore with members like Michael Joseph, Esther Ramani and J. Gowri Shivakumar after the Special Interest Group in IATEFL wrote of them. The group was a model of its kind and worked in a very democratic, non-hierarchical way to discuss issues. It had a bottom-up approach. CPD brings me back full circle. We were looking at observation and supervision today within a CPD framework.

Srivastava: How important are observation and supervision in a discussion of CPD and classroom pedagogy?

Bolitho: The Minds Project is a perfect example. Within the ambit of CPD the different purposes of observation and a principled approach to supervision has a potential impact on professional development.

Pillai: Outcome-based teaching has become a central concern of education today. Given that, what would you include as imperatives in classroom pedagogy?

Bolitho: Teachers must know where they are headed and therefore outcomes and predicting destinations is important. At the same time they should not be obsessed with outcomes only. The process of getting to the destination is more important. One should not privilege the product over the process. Observation and supervision is part of that process.

Srivastava: You have travelled widely and have interacted with scholars from around the world. In institutes other than teacher training institutes, what are the other segments of higher education where observation and supervision help?

Bolitho: Apart from teacher training institutes, institutions like the Higher Education Academy in Britain demand that there should be a mandatory observation exercise by a peer every year. This is followed by a written report on the exercise. Such initiatives are indicative of a learning organization.

Pillai: Observation and supervision are much more complex than they appear to be. What are the inherent challenges?

Bolitho: I look at these challenges as four dilemmas that a practitioner must negotiate to derive value from the exercise. The first one is to understand that we all carry 'Baggage' about our own views on quality teaching and become judgemental about others' methods. One must consciously make a package of all these critical voices in one's head and leave it outside the door before entering a room to carry out an observation exercise. It is not easy but it comes with self-discipline and practice. The second dilemma is the 'Perception Gap'. By this I mean the different perspectives people have to the same event. The teacher's point of view could be at variance with that of the observer's. This can be minimized by dialogue and raising of awareness by the parties concerned. If handled well, it can be a good opportunity for mutual learning. Such a strategy would allow the observer to go deeper into critical moments in the session than look at the particular class as an artefact.

The third dilemma is the 'Impact of the Observer's Presence in the Classroom'. What is the status he should be accorded? Is the observer to be included in the equation as a guest, an assessor or a participant in the event? Would it not then distract the learners and also make the teacher's performance stilted? Is there a need for the observer to be always present? The last dilemma is 'Feedback'. It is a vital part of the whole exercise. The directiveness of feedback is normally proportional to the experience of the teacher who was observed. A fresh young teacher would be impatient with expectations, whereas an experienced teacher would look at it more for validation or reiteration. In any case, feedback has to be negotiated wisely and should be based on questioning techniques. The observer must not be abrupt, judgemental or conclusive in his feedback. He must not lose sight of the fact that he also has a mentoring role to play.

Pillai: You mentioned Donald Freeman's seminal article on observation (TESOL Quarterly, Vol. 16, No. 1, March 1982) in this context. Can you please elaborate on that?

Bolitho: Freeman makes a distinction between training and development. He sees them as two ends of a continuum wherein training imparts more of skills while development addresses the whole person by way of personal and professional growth. It is here that he discusses three possible approaches to observation: the Supervisory Approach which is largely prescriptive and therefore addresses training issues for the observed teacher; the Alternatives Approach which is more equitable and non-evaluative; and lastly the Non-Directive Approach where the observer uses the counselling approach and becomes an 'understander' or a catalyst in facilitating self-enquiry in the teacher.

Srivastava: Supervision generally means 'having an overview of classroom teaching'. It is also supposed to be a non-threatening strategy. Is it really so?

Bolitho: It is the business of the supervisor to take the threat out of supervision. Clarity about the focus of the observation exercise and pre- lesson and post-lesson dialogues will help.

Srivastava: What is the difference between observation and supervision?

Bolitho: It is easy to locate observation in supervision. It is one way of talking to a teacher.

Srivastava: How can observation, supervision and classroom teaching happen in a collaborative manner?

Bolitho: It is a real fight to banish subjectivity from the exercise. Baggage is always a danger. But we must keep trying to keep it at bay.

Srivastava: In Delhi University, where we have been teaching English for the last 20 years or so, formal observation of classroom teaching has never happened. Our observers and supervisors are our students. How do you respond to this?

Bolitho: Students know how to differentiate between good teaching from the not so good. But it is important to look at feedback from the whole student body and not rely on any one isolated response. That would give you a skewed response.

Srivastava: Isn't observation and supervision a top-down approach with an inbuilt hierarchy in it?

Bolitho: Teachers have to understand that it is a collaborative venture which is going to benefit them in the long run. The classroom cannot be seen as a closed-door domain. Gibbs and Habeshaw (1989) and King (1983), talk about the advantages of post-observation feedback procedures.

Srivastava: The last decade has brought new challenges in learning platforms like Virtual Learning Environments (VLE), E-learning, E-classrooms, etc. Some claim that this has shaken the fulcrum on which classroom learning rests: face-to-face interaction, observation and supervision. How do we negotiate this 'E' menace?

Bolitho: E-learning can never replace face-to-face learning. E-learning compulsions are quite different in as much as it offers flexibility, logistic advantages and wider participation. E-learning gives opportunities to those learners who can't physically come to attend classes. In Norwich Institute for Language Education (NILE), we use blended learning wherein face-to-face sessions are supported by online tutorials. This I feel is an advantageous model.

Srivastava: Don't you think that observation, supervision and feedback are still some challenges that this platform needs to overcome.

Bolitho: You are right and that is why I say that it can never replace face-to-face learning.

13

Knowing 'Theory' Will Not Automatically Ensure Quality Assessment

Rama Mathew

Interviwed by Lina Mukhopadhyay

Lina Mukhopadhyay: What according to you, is assessment and how can it be carried out in class to support learning?

Rama Mathew: Assessment within the school/college curriculum deals broadly with summative assessment (SA) and formative assessment (FA). SA is assessment of the sum-total of learning in a given year, i.e. the 'product' of learning while FA reflects a commitment to understand and support learning during the 'process' of learning. SA could also be seen as externally conducted in that the Board/University takes responsibility to conduct a common test(s) across schools/colleges for purposes of comparability and certification. FA falls under the purview of teachers and students. In this sense we can contrast the two modes in terms of the *purpose* of assessment and also in terms of *who* is involved in conducting the assessment.

Mukhopadhyay: Formative assessment, more often than not, seems to be imitating the summative assessment format. Do you think that teachers are allowed to design formative assessments independently?

Earlier published in *FORTELL* Issue No. 35 (July 2017).

Mathew: Probably this perception, more common in schools than at the tertiary level, arises because school boards are increasingly 'fixing' test formats to such an extent that teachers need to hardly think or work on their own about what to test and how to test; it's all pre-determined by the board. This probably is because it is believed that teachers are not capable of designing their own assessment tools let alone construct suitable questions/test items.

Mukhopadhyay: Is this the reason why we focus so much on content-based assessment in language classrooms in India?

Mathew: Content-based assessment, i.e. asking questions on already taught content (when the content is supposed to be only the means for fine-tuning your language in a language classroom) emanates from a prescribed textbook (PTB) approach. There is no easy escape from content-based testing in a PTB system: whenever the prescribed texts (poems, stories, plays, etc.) are not overtly tested, it is seen as 'outside' the PTB and is considered a waste of time and resources. I remember, when CBSE implemented the communicative approach and introduced the 'Interact in English' series, the Board desperately resisted too much outside content in the exam papers. The plea, then, was: how are the weak learners going to pass the exam? And interestingly, even teachers, at least those who did not receive adequate orientation to the approach, saw teaching the 'Main Course Book' as a waste of time, as there were not too many 'direct' questions students could prepare for from the exam point of view. No one saw the value of practising all the four skills in engaging ways and sharpening their skills in the process, which this book provided ample opportunities for; parents understandably opposed unnecessary emphasis on listening and speaking skills which were not formally tested then. Clearly the high-stakes final exam had a powerful washback on what happened in the classroom.

Mukhopadhyay: Making language tests based on the prescribed textbook seems to be the norm. Is it in anyway related to the idea of maintaining uniformity in test formats across schools?

Mathew: The answer is multifold and is also intertwined: PTBs allow uniformity across schools and define the limits of the syllabus which is otherwise elusive for a teacher. This way teachers are held accountable: exams that are based on a given PTB can be easily seen to be within or outside the syllabus. Further, teachers do not have to select materials on a daily basis for which most of them would not have the necessary skills. We know that critiquing a set of materials, adapting them and using them according to varying student levels and interests is a highly specialized area and needs training. Therefore, PTBs actually serve as shortcuts to the otherwise complex task that every teacher is not ready for. There is also the issue of access to good and authentic materials; not every teacher has the time or the ability to find appropriate materials for the given syllabus. So what we have in essence is a standardized system where 'experts' put together a textbook based on the syllabus and the exam stems out of that and given these two fixed entities, the teacher ensures that students are prepared to answer exam questions so that they score high marks/grades.

Mukhopadhyay: What is the role of the teacher in all this preparation—is it only to ensure that students answer questions?

Mathew: The teacher is merely an assembly line worker and students 'products' that emerge at the end of the assembly line: the more uniform (all high scorers with a few exceptions) they are, the better for the system to justify the whole process. I know I'm presenting a very gloomy picture and not all teachers are assembly-line functionaries. But given that the system is based on an input-output model, there is very little we can do about what happens in the classroom, 'black-box' as it is often called. That explains why we do not interrogate what teachers and students actually do inside the classroom.

Mukhopadhyay: As part of this 'gloomy' scenario are we also not undermining the potential of assessment in addition to treating teachers as 'assembly line workers'?

Mathew: Assessment often fulfils a *fait-accompli* function. Although it has enormous possibilities to give ample evidence of *where* one is at a given stage, *what* one wants to achieve and *how* one can go *where* they wish to, we seldom exploit it fully. CCE (Continuous Comprehensive Evaluation) for example, that CBSE introduced (and has now withdrawn) is an example of how something that has an enormous potential is under-utilized or even distorted quite often.

Mukhopadhyay: How did CCE influence teachers and what kind of tests were they required to create?

Mathew: For the first time probably the term *formative assessment* became part of teachers' active vocabulary in this scheme and it intended to break away from the typical 'unit test' concept and provided for assessing students' learning continually through not just a paper-pencil test but various methods such as quizzes, assignments, projects, portfolios, pair and group work and so forth. Given the magnitude of operations and the need to maintain some sort of uniformity for purposes of comparability across schools, the Board required every school to follow the scheme of four FAs and two SAs during the two terms in an academic year. The SAs are typically paper-pencil tests with a given break-up for reading, writing and grammar and literature, which is based on a PTB. CBSE also set aside 20 marks for assessing listening and speaking carried out at the school level, for which guidelines and very often actual tasks were provided.

Mukhopadhyay: Given this fantastic structure proposed through the concept of CCE, are there no doubts regarding its implementation?

Mathew: Actually many questions arise in this context: Are teachers using a variety of assessment tools as part of FA? If so, how well are they being designed and used? What skill(s) do they focus on? We know from experience that good assessment requires extensive training and practice. Are teachers equipped to handle this with a reasonable level of sophistication? Even as they learn on the job, is continuing support provided? The short (3-5 days) training in assessment that some teachers might have received is definitely not adequate. Therefore what appears as a 'modern' scheme, while it is definitely an improvement over the earlier traditional unit-test model, is not achieving its full potential. I don't have any research evidence to claim its efficacy one way or other, but from what teachers report generally, there seems to be a range of 'not satisfactory' to 'quite good' practice that exists. And this seems to depend on whether a given school expects its teachers to follow sound assessment practices or not. I can say one thing with some certainty: I have met many teachers who admit to their 'ignorance' of how FA should be carried out; worse still, they are not aware of what actually FA is all about. The very impressive scheme and the teachers' manual for CCE seem to be just a policy document that outlines everything that is desirable, but what happens in reality is a far cry from what is envisaged.

Having said that, I must now mention that CBSE has withdrawn the CCE scheme and introduced what they call 'Uniform Scheme of Assessment' which does not talk anymore about FA and SA but Periodic Assessment (20 per cent) comprising periodic tests worth 10 marks, notebook submission and enrichment activities for 5 marks each. The yearly exam gets a weight of 80 per cent. I'd call this move regressive, if only to maintain uniformity across 18,000 odd schools across the country.

The situation I described earlier about not entrusting the teacher with any responsibility and supporting him/her with adequate training is now further strengthened. The entire concern seems to be about making report cards comparable across schools for easy mobility of children from one school/state to another. I'm quite concerned that other states will now whole-heartedly or half-heartedly follow this pattern.

Mukhopadhyay: Let me move to a slightly different but related area now. What about the assessment systems in colleges and universities in India? Are there similar problems to what we face at the school level?

Mathew: It is actually a different story with college/university teachers. There are in my view two types available: one, a very traditional category where 'old type' paper-pencil tests are used that usually test knowledge and understanding of prescribed texts and some 'stock' essay/paragraph questions peppered with some discrete grammar and vocabulary items. The more recent or new ones are those that try to make it as communicatively oriented as possible; this is available in some more recently set up progressive universities or engineering colleges/universities where students are assessed on reading, writing, vocabulary and grammar items. To what extent such tests manage to test students' ability in those skills they claim to, varies from one situation to another. It can vary from *not at all/hardly* to *quite well* on a validity or effectiveness scale.

Mukhopadhyay: So does that mean that in the more progressive universities listening and speaking also get assessed, given that they are an integral part of everyday communication?

Mathew: Almost invariably students are not tested on speaking and listening skills in a formal way as they are tested on reading and writing skills in a test-situation. However, they are assessed on these skills especially in the more progressive contexts in a seminar mode through PPTs, group presentations, and so forth. This then is tested internally, by their teachers and usually counts towards their final grade. The English proficiency courses offered to undergraduate students at Ambedkar University, Delhi is an example.

Mukhopadhyay: Can we say that these communicative modes of assessment help teachers capture 'growth' in learning the second language?

Mathew: Well, I would say that teachers can see 'growth' in students' performance if they wish to. Because put simply, whatever the criteria for assessment, if student X is making progress from assessment 1 to 2 to 3, then it is clearly visible in terms of marks or grades. Also, teachers have a good sense of how their students are doing, through their observations and interactions with students. But very often, this goes unrecorded or unacknowledged. It's even better if their performance is described qualitatively: Did the student(s) make fewer grammatical errors, or was their presentation more coherent? In what way? Did it have a more effective introduction and conclusion and so forth. One can clearly see a progression, in the context of the criteria used. More importantly this change in their performance should be perceptible to students, provided we decide to involve them in the assessment design and process, i.e. what tasks to use, what criteria and the assessing process itself.

Mukhopadhyay: Please give us some examples of formative assessment.

Mathew: I would like to share my experience of teaching the course on Evaluation at the BEd level and also the course on Qualitative Research Methods to MPhil and PhD scholars at CIE (Delhi University) where I worked. With BEd students, we spent the initial several hours examining critically what assessment practices they had been subjected to as students, both in school and college. This provided the basis for thinking of and practising 'new' approaches such as portfolios, open book exams, writing as a process, etc. What made the course effective was that they, as students, experienced first-hand all the 'new' approaches that we were learning about, to be used with their students later on.

Mukhopadhyay: Give us some more details of how the students were supported.

Mathew: On the research methodology course, the MPhil and PhD scholars worked in teams of 2-3 on a small research study, and wrote it up with continuous support from each other and me, the tutor, and learnt about researching, collaboration, academic writing which involved 2-3 drafts with peer-feedback and all of that. Peer-review involved looking for a good introduction and a conclusion, coherence, hedging, the rationale for headings and subheadings, the language used and other features that they found relevant. By the end of the entire process, they produced a 'paper' that in 50 per cent of the cases could be considered for publication. They found the writing part quite tough but enjoyable as they could see progress towards a full-fledged paper. Peer-review, editing, giving and receiving feedback and doing at least 3 drafts were all required for a satisfactory grade for this assignment. That was the only way I could ensure everyone went through the process to understand what academic writing involved. During the final 'test' they critiqued their own assignment from the early stages to the end and graded themselves on it. I couldn't have taught a course on 'Academic Writing' without the mini-research study providing the base. On the whole it was very satisfying and a huge learning experience for all of us.

Mukhopadhyay: You must have guided quite a few doctoral dissertations on assessment. Does any example come to your mind where growth is systematically captured and reported?

Mathew: Nupur Samuel from the University of Delhi did a research study that involved young adults in learning to write. Students refined a set of criteria for assessing writing tasks and in fact it was when they understood what those criteria actually meant that they started improving. Of course the research study was set up in such a way that it enabled involvement of students gradually and empowered them to take responsibility for their learning.

Mukhopadhyay: You have told us a lot about assessment at the school and college level, and also a bit about research that you have guided in the area. Can I take you back to formative assessment and link that with training? Would you say that teachers can practise formative assessment only if they are trained?

Mathew: Assessment is all about practice: a good scheme can only go up to a point. Whether teachers who have to concretize it in live classroom contexts are equipped to handle it, including self/peer-assessment and how they feed the evidence back to their future teaching work to improve learning are all easily said than practised. Therefore, FA which is the teacher's responsibility is much more complex and demanding than SA which can be externally designed and managed. For this to happen the single most important component is training in assessment. Training programmes that offer courses or modules on classroom methodology seldom have a full module on assessment. CIEFL (EFL University now) where I worked for several years, had a course on assessment as an optional course that teachers could opt out of. But a teacher is by default an assessor and can't opt out of it. Even the most famous BEd programme at the Department of Education where I taught had the course on evaluation as an elective and now in the two-year programme I understand it has half the weight of a methodology course. But why? What is the rationale? My colleague who teaches courses on assessment at the Department in Delhi University remarked quite seriously: 'Where is the need for teachers to learn about assessment? Anyway students have to pass!' We have trivialized this field so much that we will have to work quite hard to redeem it.

Mukhopadhyay: I agree that it has been trivialized. Any way out of this problem?

Mathew: We will need to professionalize assessment in a way we have not done so far. We will need to spend our time, effort and money on assessment training. When we shy away from it, the results are dangerous and harm the education system seriously, beyond repair. A last comment on this issue: at the tertiary level, no training of any sort exists and we can imagine how teachers stumble and learn things on the job. A recent thesis on how college teachers conceptualize learning and assessment throws light on many of these issues (see Violet Macwan's thesis from Delhi University).

Mukhopadhyay: Undoubtedly formative assessment design and practice is challenging. What are your suggestions for teachers?

Mathew: First of all as I said earlier, teachers need one thing for which there is no substitute or short cut possible i.e. training in assessment. While it doesn't have to be face-to-face for a given number of days, it will have to be a planned, structured and a hands-on programme where teachers can together read about, discuss, design and construct assessments for different levels of learners. There are many MOOCs available, for example: Designing Assessments to Measure Student Outcomes (https://www.futurelearn.com/courses/assessments-student-outcomes). Teachers in a school or college can form a friendly group and decide what they want to learn in assessment: is it about how they can monitor student progress in the classroom; or developing test items to assess different skills, i.e. listening, reading, writing and speaking; or developing appropriate criteria for marking productive skills, i.e. speaking and writing? The area is pretty large and one has to go about it in small steps. A very important dimension about teachers making such efforts together is that they can try out new ideas in their classroom and share their experience with others and this way engage in action research. I would like to re-emphasize that assessment is all about practice. All the theoretical concepts come alive in practice; knowing 'theory' will not automatically ensure quality assessment.

Mukhopadhyay: Do learners have a role in formative assessment as well?

Mathew: Yes, a crucial dimension is to involve learners. When you ask them about what kind of assessments they like, and how they would like to be assessed, you will be amazed at how much they know and how well they can assess themselves or their peers; of course you will need to monitor them unobtrusively and guide them as they progress. We often feel that when we leave assessment to students, they might cheat or inflate their marks or they don't know enough to be able to assess which is in fact the teacher's job. Some of it might even be true, but when you create an atmosphere of mutual trust and bonhomie, part of what we call 'learner-centred pedagogy', you will see that children of all age groups can be ethical, trustworthy, and honest and more importantly competent. In one study that I carried out long ago, I found that students of Grade 9 were more 'critical' of their writing than me and they always gave themselves at least one score less than what I did.

Mukhopadhyay: If teachers decide to get help from assessment experts in training, will that help?

Mathew: I'd say that when teachers get together and decide how they might want to go about training themselves, they might want an assessment 'expert' to guide or mentor them: it's always possible to call them in, but be very sure of what you want them to do and at what stage of your group's work you want their inputs. Given a chance, experts will give you good lectures on how to do credible assessment but it is seldom useful for actual work. And these days 'experts' are available with a click on the mouse—there is so much help available in the form of YouTube videos, TED talks, PPTs and articles that we just need to spend some time on the computer. But one thing—I've found that it's fun to learn together and share.

14

Professional Development Needs to be Interactive for Impact

Shobha Sinha

Interviewed by Prachi Kalra

Prachi Kalra: Let me begin by asking you a very general question, how do you envision Continuous Professional Development (CPD) and what value do you see for it in the teaching profession?

Shobha Sinha: If you don't develop professionally, what happens in the teaching profession? I mean, when we talk about teaching, we are conscious that after a while a certain staleness can come into it. I always say to my students that the punishment that you have of poor teaching is right there—you can see it in the faces of your students. So there is really no choice, you need to have professional development. The other thing is that in the field of education and pedagogy or even a subject area that you are teaching there is extensive growth which you should know about and which you should contribute to. Otherwise you would be teaching yesterday's content and knowledge. So, for very obvious reasons it is not a matter of choice, you really have to keep going with CPD.

But I just want to share a personal story with you. One of the areas I teach is a course in literacy, which I am absolutely passionately interested in. I really want more students to

---

Earlier published in *FORTELL* Issue No. 37 (July 2018).

understand it because it is still not widely studied in India. About 10 years ago, one year I just felt that I did not even want to go to class and it was just repetitive and I said, 'My goodness! Is something wrong with me that I don't even care about class?' And just after that I went on study leave where I was doing research on early literacy in Jharkhand. When I came back, and I had to start teaching right away, I noticed that my classes dramatically changed. There was a lot of energy in class, excitement—there were examples, there were things to talk about—and I was willing to listen much more. This is just a small example to show that if you really want to teach effectively there is no choice about professional development.

Kalra: You have been a school teacher, you teach at the university now, you have taught courses in Literacy, Reading and Writing. Do you feel that there is a difference between say teaching at the school level or teaching at the university level and would you say that therefore continuous professional development in both these contexts would be different or should take a different shape?

Sinha: The demands sometimes can be different. I mean, again for very obvious reasons, there are differences in the volume of teaching that you do in school and in college; how much responsibility the student takes and how much responsibility you take, those things differ. But I don't think that we differ very much in terms of the need to keep up with the development of ideas or the need for freshness of ideas. I think CPD is equally important for both fields.

Kalra: Talking about freshness of ideas, how do you think CPD could engage with that? Very often when we talk about CPD, it takes the form of training, inviting experts and then training teachers. Do you think that this is a good way of looking at CPD? What could be other ways of bringing in freshness of ideas, of empowering teachers, giving them the ability to look at their own classrooms and learn from that?

Sinha: The most important question is just how much do

we understand the nature of our profession itself. We may understand it from our own experiences, but how much is it a part of the discourse? For instance, dealing with bureaucracy, which all of us do whether at school or university level. If you understand the nature of the profession, there are many things you will understand. What does the teaching hour mean? During that one hour you might be teaching or you might be having a serious discussion. So, there are many aspects of the teaching hour. It's only when you teach, that you really understand how staleness comes in when you look at the teaching hour only in one way. I don't know if we have done enough of a job to make people understand this. At one level we protest against rules and notifications, but at another level we just go along instead of really questioning bureaucratic perceptions of teaching.

I'll give an example, as teacher educators we make school visits to observe students. That's also a form of teaching; it's just that you are not giving a lecture but you are sitting at the back of the classroom and observing student-teacher teach. Now you have done it so you do realize that when you go and observe a certain number of students it's a very draining experience. And we keep doing it year after year. Now if you understand the nature of the teaching profession, you would realize that it is very important to give a break in between and go back refreshed. If you don't, you destroy the teacher, you destroy the programme, and most importantly, hurt the students. So the growth and the well-being of the teacher is very important because your programme is only as good as that. You can't worry about students independently without worrying about teachers. I think we lack in our concern for teachers.

Also, empowerment is not something which we can offer to someone on a plate. You can just create an enabling environment. A few years ago, I attended a training programme, and people did care about it [creating an enabling environment] but the policies were very top-down.

The organizers wanted us to train teachers in early language and literacy in three days. I have taught that for years and, tell me, what do you achieve in three days? I find this whole cramming thing very problematic. Just because all the topics have been covered, does not mean everyone has understood.

The other thing is, why aren't we asking the teachers about their point of view, their learning? Do they have something to share? And it's the same with refresher courses. Even if it's a good programme for three weeks, we could envision it differently so that there is empowerment and people bring their own ideas to share. It should be interactive in nature, more of a dialogue. Of course, we can invite experts, but the need should be dictated by teachers, and not a top-down approach. Let me tell you a funny incident. At a three-day CPD programme, where from morning to evening resource persons came and talked about something or the other, a colleague kept writing furiously. So, I asked her, 'What were you taking notes about?' She said, 'You know I have finally caught up with all the letters that I had to write to relatives!' So something in me just rebels at the thought of people coming in and just dictating things to you.

I am not saying that all of us can't learn. And, that's another aspect of the teacher which is very important, that you should be willing to learn, but I think that at some time we should start talking about an enabling context for CPD. Development doesn't take place in three days or three weeks, it happens only through dialogue. Have a dialogue! Teachers should be on the panel talking about their experiences. One thing that I have been recommending at different forums is that there should be a research component in each college—research not to get 10 or 15 points for publishing—but to engage with ideas, to talk to other scholars about ideas that don't grow in these workshops. It is in the corridors when you regroup while having coffee, when you talk about a book you might have read, that dialogue happens. But, first of all, you should have that book to read! There should be an inclination, availability and mingling, and an environment where you can talk about it.

Kalra: In which case would you say that one very important aspect of CPD might be enabling teachers to form their own professional networks which we lack in India, we don't seem to believe in them. All CPD seems to happen in the form of 'top-down' training modules, as you said, which happen sporadically over a certain number of days and then we are done with them. How do you think teacher networks can be built, where teachers can support each other and engage in collaborative research or in getting together and discussing issues that they feel concerned about?

Sinha: See, there are again two sides to it. You might have been teaching for a long time, there have been many developments in your field, so I am not saying that you don't have new things to learn. But I object just to the fixed structuring of that. With new ideas, initially, there is considerable resistance. Unless you engage and you are willing to listen and talk about different ideas, and admit that you too don't know everything, you will not learn. Teachers also need to be open to new ideas. It needs to be a true dialogue and not a fake one. Again, whatever CPD model you choose don't try to do everything, as a banking model of teaching. You could talk about one point and let people try it out and come back and talk about what happened when they tried to implement it and discuss and critique it. Then there is much more investment in that CPD programme. Otherwise you can get a lot of resistance. Just because teachers were physically present over there and nodded their heads doesn't lead to continuous professional development.

Empowerment has to be enabled, there has to be a dialogue, and, you're right, we do not have strong enough networks. When we do organize conferences for CPD at the university level, we just drain our energy in figuring out all the details, from the quality of the academic papers, to thinking about what kind of food to order, and other practical things. And that is quite draining! In the US, for example, professional networks are very strong and I know that it's unfair to compare our country to theirs, but we can take some lessons from them. Their organizational networks are fairly big and they have funding for conferences and arrangements are made so that you are not dealing with all the details, but only with the academic part. Here, it has all become a very mechanical culture frankly, if you ask me. So, I think that networks need to be strengthened and many different level activities need to take place but I think, very importantly, that members need space to go and discuss things. That dialogue among teachers is very important where you can just meet to talk about your difficulties or even know that others are in the same boat.

Kalra: I teach in the Department of Education in college and I know that most of my colleagues in the other departments do not really come with an understanding of pedagogy. Do you think that at the university level CPD might address some of these concerns? What could be important elements that need to be addressed for teachers at the college/university level?

Sinha: I think this point is very valid because teaching is teaching no matter at what level you are doing it. However, in education while we do talk about pedagogy and assessment, but when it comes to applying it to our students fully, we are unable to do it. During our moderation meetings, I remember, one faculty had given six assignments for 15 points. So if you have 15 points for your internal assessment for a fifty mark paper, remember the student has more papers, and yours is just a part of it. Because we like to be a busy department, we like to give a lot of assignments, but that is totally against the whole principle of assessment. We need to think about the principles of assessment and be aware of new ideas in the field, because authority comes also from knowing those things. Merely knowing about assessment doesn't mean it translates into teaching.

However, as far as other departments are concerned, I think your point is very valid. There should be discussions on assessment and pedagogy. What form it should take, I really don't know. Like other countries, we need to have a course on composition. For instance, you could have a refresher course on teaching clarity in writing, instead of a refresher course where multiple things are being dealt with. A more focused course where a group meets to discuss teaching and then reads certain things together and talks about them, maybe that could work. I remember when I was a beginning faculty in the US, we used to have a lunch meeting once every week about different aspects of undergraduate teaching. Sometimes, you might have very rebellious undergraduate students and you are not sure how to assess them or how they might respond to their assessment. So, we would talk about that or about what we could read but the meeting grew out of our needs. Throughout the term we had these meetings and we could mention them in our annual report. We had the freedom to talk, sometimes complain, but also actually learn from each other and also from the students. I think that every model doesn't have to be very rigid. As I said, corridors are the best places for growth.

Kalra: One thing I feel is very important at the university level now, is the ability of the teachers to understand the diversity in their classrooms because universities are increasingly diverse places. So, do you think that there is some way CPD could address that or enable teachers to understand the diversity in their classrooms?

Sinha: That is very important, but again if you had, let's say, a three-day workshop and somebody came and told you about its various components, would it help? One thing is just acknowledging a field of study and get some terms which you can glibly use and completely another thing to transform your pedagogy. If you want to focus more on impact then again it has to be more interactive, it has to be spread over time. And it does not need to be very focused or intense. Maybe you can meet two days or something and talk about ideas, read together, but I think it needs to be spread out to sink in.

And I think the point you raise is very valid because when I started teaching in CIE many times in my tutorial class or in my school visits I would have visually challenged students and I really didn't know what to do. I needed more in-depth understanding of those issues but also about various kinds of diversities that you have in your classroom and how you deal with them to develop that level of sensitivity. I think that applies to all departments—they should be thinking and talking about diversity, there should be an environment for it. Of course, we have access to lectures and scholars coming in and they are useful. I am not saying that they aren't, but training courses or workshops are often just so spread out and ritualistic. I do have a problem with them because people attend then for commercial purposes and that should not be the spirit.

Kalra: Do you think it's a good idea for, say the Department of Education and its various pedagogy experts to have that kind of synergy with the other departments at the university and thereby to form an exchange where pedagogical ideas get addressed and then feed into classroom teaching? Do you think it is a feasible idea?

Sinha: Can the other departments accept that? I'm not sure. But I think the first challenge is to understand that there is lot more involved in classroom teaching than just going in and delivering the lecture. So, those are the things that we need to think about. As I said earlier, just knowing about pedagogical topics doesn't mean that we do implement them in our classrooms. I gave you that example of assessment. But the awareness that there are many issues to think about, I feel that is very important. Teacher empowerment is not just a fashionable word to use because teachers can have their own ways of resistance, and in a way I sympathize with that because of the way teachers get treated. But if the need for learning new ideas comes more from within and there is more dialogue, it's not as if we can't share materials and ideas. And it's not like the Department of Education alone has experts.

Kalra: One last question! This is a question that lies close to my heart. I have in my readings come across what are called 'Reading Experts', especially in the US, through Continuous Professional Development that they have. So, teachers who become Reading Experts very often work with struggling readers and writers in schools, and are seen as reading specialists. Do you think that this is something that we could learn from and develop?

Sinha: First of all do we even recognize 'reading' as an area of expertise? Actually, in the Master's programme in the US, Reading Specialists study a certain number of courses to become that. It is not as simple as a few hours of CPD. I recall that teachers used to come back to the university to take a full course, like I remember once I taught a course in the 'Foundations of Reading' and there were many teachers who had years of experience and they took the full course. I think that is more effective than taking a three-day workshop on reading. It's so counter-intuitive to people. Whatever professional development we do, we should do it with a more sustained engagement. We are fooling ourselves if we think that in one day we can learn all about assessment or whatever the topic is. Another thing I want to say is that no development can take place without real space and real time. The enabling context—we really need to think about that. We are very careless about protecting our time.

I would like to add one more thing without you asking about it. I had read about a leading college in Delhi University and there was this scathing piece by the Principal, where he gave this caricature of a University Professor who dashes off to this conference and then to another and writes a paper and isn't worried about the students. Let me tell you, that without your own growth and learning, and being in the position to produce knowledge, you are not going to be a very good teacher. What spaces are we providing for that? For instance, if you are teaching English, let's say in school, and you never get a chance to read a book, how effective are you going to be? Maybe you won't teach that very book. And it's tough to put your finger on it. I might read a book for another purpose and because I really enjoyed it I might use it for teaching 'Marginalization'. If I hadn't read it, I couldn't have used it. So, to be on the cutting edge of research and knowledge building, you have to actually engage with new ideas and you can't do that without having time for it. But having time is looked down upon, you are supposed to be always busy and ready when somebody calls you to do this or that. Especially for us teachers, we need to realize that space and time need to be protected. And, maybe in spite of that many people won't work, but actually many people would work! We are too busy trying to catch people out to think about an enabling environment.

Future Directions

15

Popular Culture and Media Studies Comprise the Very Ontology of Literary Studies

Saugata Bhaduri

Interviewed by Rachna Sethi

Rachna Sethi: The debate whether English departments should be dealing with language or/and literature is an old one. Increasingly people feel that we are headed towards 'end of pure literatures' and we need to focus on language teaching. How do you respond to it, especially as CES (Centre for English Studies) is located in the School of Language, Literature and Culture Studies?

Saugata Bhaduri: There are two issues raised in this question, both extremely pertinent to the discipline of English Studies. I will take them up one after the other.

To the question whether English departments should be teaching English language or English literature, the answer is obviously 'both'. However, the problem arises when there is a conflation of these two very different mandates of an English department. As much as literature may have been historically used to teach English language, language teaching and imparting literary responsiveness are altogether different projects. The objective of the former is to arm a student, with little or no proficiency in the language, with instrumental

---

Earlier published in *FORTELL* Issue No. 24 (May 2012).

(more often than not, non-literary) working skills in English, while the objective of the latter is to equip a student, already in command of the language, with aesthetic and critical sensibility, which may run completely contrary to the normative instrumentalization presumed in the former. A department of English has to perform both these tasks, but neither displace one with the other, nor confuse the two as being part of the same exercise and aimed at the same audience.

Regarding the second question about the 'end of pure literatures', if by 'literature' we refer only to printed matter, we must understand that printing is a very recent, less than 600-year-old phenomenon. 'Literature', as a process of mass-circulated narrative discursivization, pre-existed print technology (otherwise Kalidasa and Homer should not be considered literary) and will continue to survive, in spite of the imminent 'end' of print in the digital age. In fact, 'literature' has become even more relevant in these information-driven times of ours, because now we are surrounded and guided by discourses more than ever before. It is just that the media of articulation of these ubiquitous discourses are different from the temporary medium of print that we often erroneously associate 'literature' solely with.

Both the issues referred to above are, as has been rightly presumed in the question, of special relevance to our Centre, located as it is in the School of Language, Literature and Culture Studies. The existence of 'Culture Studies' within the scope of our School entails that the study of English here is not restricted to printed literature alone, the second problem addressed above. And it being located within the School of 'Languages' also includes English language teaching within our purview, the first of the two problems. And, the fact that, while our advanced MA and MPhil/PhD programmes obviously do not include a language-teaching component, our Centre is located in a School of Languages, with undergraduate students with varying degrees of proficiency in English, expects us to impart 'language' training in English too.

Our Centre has been able to fulfil this dual mandate successfully, precisely by separating these two objectives. Thus, we run two parallel programmes, so to say—the usual literary and cultural courses for students already proficient in the language and who instead need to be inculcated into critical thought and aesthetic sensibility, and the very successful Remedial English programme for all students of the University, who are deficient in the language and would rather require language skills—resulting in there being two departments of English, as it were, in JNU: the CES which imparts knowledge in literature and culture in English, and the English Language Cell, administered jointly by our Centre and the Centre of Linguistics, and located directly under the central university administration, which imparts English language training.

In short, it is first, in a recognition of the dual mandate that English as a discipline has in India and the realization that there needs to be a separation of the two—in terms of target groups, resource persons involved, and pedagogic strategies engaged—and secondly, in the acceptance that literary studies historically has not been—and cannot be all the more now—restricted to print media alone that one can do real justice to the two very different issues raised in the question.

Sethi: JNU's Centre for English Studies has been among the foremost in the country to deconize British writing in teaching of literature in India, and in 'creating new canons' through its syllabi. How is this progressive outlook carried out today in terms of courses conducted at the Centre?

Bhaduri: While you are right in recognizing our Centre as having been at the vanguard in questioning the erstwhile canon of English Studies in India, the fact that your question also charges us with 'creating new canons' points out the problems inherent in such an exercise. The objective of critical thought cannot be to displace one canon with another, but rather to keep the flame of criticality alive that it can depart from and alter what it itself advocated earlier, when the latter may seem itself to have become the commonsense and the norm.

The decanonization process that our Centre may have initiated into English Studies from the mid-80s onwards primarily branched out in five directions—the introduction of critical political thinking to literary studies ('Literary Theory' or 'ideology-critique' in short), the introduction of literature in other Englishes (Indian, American, African, Australian, Canadian, Caribbean, etc.), the introduction of literature in Indian languages (read primarily in English translation, though), the introduction of classical Indian linguistics and aesthetics to English Studies (like Bharata, Panini, Patañjali, Bhartrhari, etc.), and the introduction of culture studies ('non-literary' modes of articulation, like folklore, film, performance, visual culture, etc.) within literary curricula. More than a quarter of a century down the line, the radical import of these shifts seem somewhat jaded, with these changes having become the new academic commonsense, the basis of what you have rightly called the 'new canon'—every English department in India now does exactly these five things. If our Centre has to retain what you have called its 'progressive outlook', it has to thus question the normativization of what it once critically stood for, and challenge its own foundations.

Needless to say, that is precisely what we are striving to do. The problem with the first of the five branchings mentioned above is that 'Literary Theory', in its commonsensical avatar at least, reduces literature to having nothing but an ideological function (that too primarily in the domain of the usual suspects—race, class, gender), at the cost of not only its hermeneutic and aesthetic functions (of cognition, of enjoyment, say), but also its excessive, transgressive and subversive roles, and its connection to overlooked means of disempowerment (caste, disability, ecology, etc). There are two problems with the second, third and fourth directions that our erstwhile decanonization took. First, universities started neglecting British literature and the erstwhile canon, resulting in a complete lack of reference to what the criticality in the radically restructured syllabi was aimed at. Second, what governed much of such restructuring was a Manichean postcolonial commonsense, which failed to recognize the complex and hybridizing matrices of colonial contact and also the fact that we (and English language and literature, indeed) have moved on from the horizon of erstwhile colonialism to the domain of globalization and new-imperialism. The problem with the fifth and final re-orientation was that new media developed radically in the last twenty years or so into cybernetic and telecommunicational modes, which the art-folklore-film-performance routine of old-media driven Culture Studies just could not cope with. If these be the problems, corollarily, the recipe to critique our own creation and continue to lead the need for evermore decanonization therefore lies in: first, focusing on domains like Dalit and Tribal Studies, Disability Studies, Ecocriticism, etc. (modes of ideology-critique under-represented in erstwhile 'Literary Theory'; second, returning to 'canonical' British literature with vengeance; third, realizing that the position of English and discursive production in the language today has little, if not nothing, to do with erstwhile colonialism and the resultant postcolonial syndrome of 'writing back to the empire' in 'national allegories'; fourth, that cyberculture and the new media have become more appropriate objects of 'literary' study today; and finally, in bringing back the element of fun and enjoyment into Literary Studies, not necessarily in an old deferential way which only considered high culture, with its enlightening and ennobling liberal humanist objective, worth studying, but in a disruptive, subversive inclusion of the profane and the popular into the classroom. These are some of the directions that our programme of English Studies and courses being currently offered at the Centre have consciously taken.

It is more than coincidental that our Centre has not offered a course in African and Australian literature for some time, or that I offer MA courses only in British literature—Renaissance drama, the rise of the novel, Romanticism, and English poetry in general. This semester, for instance, three of the nine MA courses on offer are directly on British literature—Renaissance drama, Gothic fiction, and literary Modernism; three courses—on Gandhi, on Disability Studies, and on the rhetorical construction of racism and communalism in India—bring in ideology-critique but from the perspective of altogether different contradictions, and the three courses which are ostensibly on what has been defined as the horizon of the erstwhile decanonization—Indian Writing in English, American Literature, and *Nāṭyaśāstra*—also shift their focus to include, beyond the postcolonial commonsense, texts in Indian English from the nineteenth century and contemporary genre fiction, literatures of ethnic minorities of America, and aesthetics viewed from a comparative perspective, respectively. Also, I am offering this semester an MPhil course in Popular Culture, which focuses mainly on cyberculture and the new media. All this, I believe, is symptomatic of our Centre's fresh criticality vis-à-vis its own earlier decanonizing exercise.

Sethi: Interdisciplinary studies have been the thrust of CES long before it became a buzz word in academia. Please tell us how this is encouraged at the Centre.

Bhaduri: At CES, interdisciplinarity is fostered not only through the courses that we ourselves offer—as some of the courses discussed above would indicate—but, more importantly, by encouraging students to take courses from other disciplines—History, Sociology, Political Science, Arts and Aesthetics, and Linguistics, for instance—and reciprocally welcoming students from these disciplines routinely into our courses. Of course, we are fortunate that JNU has a curricular structure that allows, and in fact encourages, students to opt for courses in other disciplines and experiment in an interdisciplinary way.

Sethi: Apart from the traditional approaches of using the disciplines of History and Philosophy to approach literature, popular media today forms an interesting entry point. What is your opinion on the use of Popular Culture in pedagogy and research of literature?

Bhaduri: Popular Culture and Media Studies comprise the very ontology of Literary Studies in today's post-print mediatized environment. Texts circulated on the new media—digital literature, cybercultural productions on social networking sites and blogs, interactive chats and messages, role playing games, fan fiction—have become not just tools, but the very object of Literary Studies in general, and English Studies in particular, today.

Sethi: Film Studies is a growing discipline with its own vocabulary, and has moved far from when 'literature' students dealt with cinematic adaptations of texts. How can it be used effectively as a cultural medium in English departments?

Bhaduri: Film Studies has been a mainstream discipline for some time now, so much so that many universities, including JNU, have full-fledged programmes in Film Studies, and it cannot be contained within adaptation studies alone. Film Studies has its own theoretical presumptions, vocabulary, and methodological universe, and it will be dangerous for an English teacher to foray into the field without adequate knowledge of the medium. That being said, one must also realize that cinema is an old medium, and now more and more people view films on other media like television, DVD players, laptops, handheld devices, improvised projection screens, etc., rather than in the theatre. And, that brings us back to the relevance of new media studies to English today, with films being just one of the several kinds of messages that have been adapted for and appropriated by the digital and cybernetic media.

Sethi: Could you please elaborate on how Cinema Studies can be used to develop critical perspectives towards contemporary Social Sciences?

Bhaduri: I think it is thought-provoking if we ask how the medium of cinema can make one become critical of Social Sciences as it is practised today. To my mind, there are two problems that beset contemporary Social Sciences—first, that, in its bid to become a 'science', it is often too empirical and relatively rare on ideas and fundamental thought; second, in its instrumentalist bid to come to social 'use', it ends up being rather austere and serious (read boring), at the cost of overlooking the (often comic) deep fissures and ruptures that underlie its very disciplinarity. Cinema—especially of the popular over-the-top potboiler sort—as an entertainment medium, can deflate, in its perfectly wasteful extravaganza, in its sheer subversive transgression of austere utility, in its foregrounding of the pleasure principle, the vain claim to observable reality and demonstrable utility that Social Science often makes.

This is of direct relevance to English Studies too. There are attempts to reduce this field—whose greatest value lies in its capability to promote disruptive and transgressive thought, Dionysian pleasure, to become a gay science, as Nietzsche would have it—to either a vocationalized utility-driven discipline, aimed at equipping a budding labour force with the tools of serving the normative new-age order, or to an instrumental hand-maiden of ideology, that can only study the victimological basis of such interpellation. Cinema, and Popular Culture in general—qua the popular, the excessive, the pleasurable—can definitely critique and expose such Apollonian and utilitarian presumptions of Social Sciences, which certain forms of English Studies also, unfortunately, have taken.

16

Academics Must Bring Caste into the Classroom Discussion

Raj Kumar

Interviewed by Gitanjali Chawla and Aarati Mujumdar

Gitanjali Chawla: For you Sir, education has been the way to emancipation, you have come a long way from Kalahandi (now Nuapada) to Delhi. Both literally and metaphorically, this journey must have been fraught with several challenges.

Raj Kumar: It was a huge leap for me, coming from an illiterate family, I happen to be the first-generation literate from my community, i.e. the first one to have passed matriculation, I did my BA and then MA from Sambhalpur University, thereafter I came to JNU, Delhi in 1991 for MPhil. There were too many problems. The first being financial, I was besieged by hostel fees, tuition fees, living expenses and there was no money coming from home, so I started giving tuitions. Basically, I am a self-dependent person. Over the years, I did very well but it was a struggle even on the academic front. My postgraduation syllabus stopped at the modern era, we did not know about postmodernism, poststructuralism etc. It was only when I came to JNU that I realized that we did not know much about the current fields of research. It was not a

---

Earlier published in *FORTELL* Issue No. 36 (January 2018). Questions were framed by Aarati Mujumdar.

burden but then it was definitely difficult for me to participate in class discussions, so I had to really work hard, sometimes 16-18 hours to catch up with my classmates. Delhi gave me many opportunities, not just in terms of academics but in everything. The culture in JNU, the kind of books available, the people around me, this was also the time we formed the United Dalit Students Forum in JNU and I was chosen as the first member. Though the journey was difficult but there were several opportunities that I availed to grow further and today I am a Professor of English at Delhi University. A lot of credit goes to my early environment and the support that I got from many of my teachers, classmates and friends.

Chawla: Language proficiency must have bothered you at some point in time?

Kumar: Yes, as far as English pronunciation was concerned, definitely. It was very different because in schools and colleges from where I came, teachers never taught us how to pronounce a particular word. So, it was self-learning, I must tell you the way we tried to learn, it went on for years, to utter a particular word in a particular form. I always tell my students even today that I am not from a public school. It took time. Even today I am learning new words, their meanings and pronunciation. Language learning is a lifelong process.

Chawla: With the baggage of caste comes a degree of self-consciousness. Do you think one can ever get rid of that baggage of self-consciousness?

Kumar: No, that will always be there. Actually, somewhere at the back, it will never go, no matter how much you may try to drive it out, it will never go.

Chawla: Is it desirable that it goes?

Kumar: No, it is not.

Chawla: You have a different vantage point!

Kumar: Yes, we talk of heterogeneity, plurality, diversity, I don't think it is desirable that everything will be the one and the same, mono culture, mono language.

Chawla: In the introduction to your translation of *Bheda,* Akhila Naik's first Odia Dalit novel, you write that socio-economic background is partly responsible for the situation that the Dalit communities are in today. Could you talk about some of the initiatives taken by the government, and other institutions like DU and JNU to bring about inclusiveness in society?

Kumar: As far as the role of the government is concerned, it is through reservations mainly and some projects. Affirmative action in the form of reservations is definitely very useful. Though implementing agencies are not really trying to implement it effectively over the years. The spirit of Indian society is essentially casteist, even DU and JNU are casteist. The spirit of Indian society is growing and will continue to do so. This will of course change over the years. More and more people from backward communities are coming forward, are participative. Even at the university level there are changes, there is progress.

Chawla: There are changes, but this is academia, allegedly progressive, yet do you think that casteism is deep-rooted even in central universities such as DU and JNU?

Kumar: Yes, this is academia! There are two ways one can understand caste, we as academia try to be radical in the public space, whenever there is a lecture, workshop, seminar or a conference, we talk about the radicalization of some of the spheres of Indian life, but when it comes to the private and the personal, we try to stick to our own customs, rigid rules, family traditions. That is why many non-Brahmanical leaders like Ambedkar and others tried to point out that it is the practices actually that people follow and not the theory. One is the idea, the idea could be radical, could be revolutionary, but what is important is how to put the ideas into practice. As Ambedkar stated, 'outcaste is a product of the caste system' and finally annihilation of caste will be there only when there are inter-caste marriages which is not happening and that is why Dalit writers ask the question: 'Will you give your daughter in marriage to my son?' I don't think Indian society is ready to accept that.

Chawla: Not yet, not now.

Kumar: Yes, not yet, the incidents of honour killings are evidence of this fact. Indian society is slowly changing but I don't think a day will come when caste will go away or completely vanish from this country.

Chawla: One can't imagine a casteless India! And also, perhaps what is disturbing is that these honour killings are not very far from mainstream centres, urban-educated academic centres, allegedly radical and progressive?

Kumar: We have seen it in DU and JNU as well. In various spheres, whether it is in appointments or selections or promotions. Even JNU, which is believed to be the most radical, is also casteist. There are many examples where caste elements are working, it is part of the system and unless and until people try to bring changes within, nothing will change. It is the 'castes of mind', Nicholas Dirks talks about the 'castes of mind'.

Chawla: Could you suggest some other measures that could be taken to bring the marginalized communities into the mainstream?

Kumar: Academics must bring caste into discussion. The first and foremost thing, that we have to do as part of larger society is to bring the discursive practices in various forums, maybe by offering courses. There is no full paper yet in Delhi University on Dalit Literature, so we as academia must find space where we can actually discuss issues related to caste. We cannot avoid bringing this discussion into classrooms, which we are presently doing. We have now been able to give some part of the undergraduate syllabus to what we call Dalit Literature. There is very little of it in MA though. I offer 4 MPhil courses dealing with Dalit Literature, besides, I have 6-7 PhD students working on Dalit literature of different languages. We cannot maybe bring actual changes by giving money to the poor and that kind of thing. Activism has its own place but, since we have space, discursive space, we can actually try to bring in different kinds of discussions. It is only with Jotiba Phule, that caste began to be discussed publicaly, but it was Ambedkar who made it an all India phenomenon. We cannot avoid caste. Secondly, we can write articles, books, contribute to magazines and implement some of the pedagogical practices.

Chawla: How can pedagogy play a pivotal role?

Kumar: Pedagogy shows how it is not one kind of approach but how diverse and different approaches could be available to a text. And since we are teachers and every year if even one or two students understand the complexities, we have made a difference. It is necessary to make students aware of caste-linked issues since they are the change agents. They are the future citizens of India, they are the ones who are going to build India.

Chawla: True, changing one's mindset is more important than how many first divisions we have churned out.

Kumar: I am happy to share that from my course, a Brahmin girl and a Dalit boy from UP got married recently despite the fact that their families were very orthodox and traditional. Moreover, they said that they were inspired by my course so there are examples that are coming in. Discussions bring in some space from which change can occur.

Chawla: Heartening indeed! In one of your articles on Dalit literature in Odia, you mention that Odia Dalits are by far the most oppressed of all. Till now why haven't these voices been more vocal than say the communities in Maharashtra, Andhra Pradesh or Gujarat?

Kumar: Yes, in the same article I mentioned that the existential condition of Odia Dalits is responsible for their oppression. The Dalit population in Odisha constitutes nearly 18 per cent of the total population, but they are marginal to the core, because economically they have to totally depend on the masters. They cannot revolt since they have to compromise for their livelihood. Secondly, we have Lord Jagannath, a pan Odia God, also an Indian phenomenon. Odia culture is dominated by the Jagannath culture. Lord Jagannath was initially a tribal God belonging to the Savara tribe. But later Savara was Hinduized and Brahmanized by the Vaishnavas and seen as the tenth avatara of Vishnu. See how Hindusim works, any kind of protesting voice is appropriated or subsumed, and Odisha is rich in protesting voices. Buddha had a dominant presence from the seventh century AD onwards, we had Buddhist Siddhas, saints who wrote protest poems condemning caste and then again from the fifteenth century onwards we had Sarala Das who was a Shudramuni, and then Panchasakha and Bhima Bhoi, a tribal poet in the nineteenth century, Phule's contemporary, who also protested against Hinduism and then in the 1970s we find some reference to caste by early Odia Dalit poets. But it is only after the 1990s when Ambedkar's writings and speeches were published and the V.P. Singh Government declared 'Social Justice and Empowerment' on the birth centenary of Ambedkar, it is only then people understood what is called 'Dalit Consciousness'. We now have full-fledged Odia Dalit Literature. My next book is on Odia Dalit Literature. There were always protests which were suppressed by dominant forces. Besides, Dalits in Odisha were too marginal to command that kind of force. It was their existential condition that prevented them from being very vocal and secondly there were no Dalit leaders like Ambedkar. There were a few minor leaders who were coopted by Congress and were actually Congress Party workers.

Chawla: What reasons can be attributed to the fact that many Odia authors are not being included in the English curriculum of university departments and colleges?

Kumar: Yes, we have now one or two, like Basudev Sunani whose poem is there. There is Jayant Mahapatra, who is also an Odia but not a Dalit poet. It actually depends on who are framing the syllabus. One has to know which writers must be included because most of the writings appear in Indian languages and are not available in English translation. That is why people may not know, for example, Basudev Sunani's poetry. We are going to publish Dalit Writing from Eastern India, a combination of Odia, Bangla, Ahamia, to be published by OUP very soon. Unless these works are available in translation, teachers in Delhi University will not be aware of them, unless they are Odia themselves, so translation plays a major role to trace the kind of writing that comes from a particular region.

Chawla: Many of the works written by early women poets were militant, aggressive and more focused on issues related to collective identity. How are Dalit women's voices different today?

Kumar: There is a trajectory, when Dalit women started writing, whether it was Bama or Sivakami in Tamil, or Baby Kamble in Marathi, Supriya Malik in Odia or others in Telugu, Bengali, etc. Dalit literature was earlier written mostly by men who were the first to get educated. When women started writing, they wrote both about the community and also about women themselves, i.e. the private space, for example. Baby Kamble's *The Prisons We Broke* is a critique of how patriarchy exists within the Dalit community. Sivakami, a Tamil novelist is very critical of how a Dalit leader becomes a sex-addict in *The Grip of Change*. He seduces not only Dalit women but also women from the upper-castes. This kind of critique is very rare, but now there are ample Dalit women voices who not only critique but give new direction to the Dalit movement. Earlier it was male dominated, but now women are forcing the Dalit leadership to reconsider Dalit women's issues, so there is a big change. For example, Sivakami's two novels, *The Grip of Change* and *The Taming of Women*, Baby Kamble's *The Prisons We Broke* and then there is Meena Kandasamy's *The Gypsy*

Goddess, and interestingly in Akhila Naik's book *Bheda*, there is a chapter called 'Mastrani' and this is his longest chapter out of seven chapters. This is a man who is trying to write from a Dalit's woman's point of view.

Chawla: Today, with the emergence of well-informed Dalit thinkers, commentators, etc. and the literature that is subsequently produced, would this literature represent class consciousness or would it get reduced to autonomous reflection and self-action resulting in the creation of new socio-cultural identities?

Kumar: The term Dalit has to be actually defined properly because originally Dalit was a term that used to refer to ex-untouchables, so there is a caste characteristic. When the Dalit Panthers movement started, the founder members like Namdeo Dhasal, a Marxist, included class within caste. For Namdeo, Dalit is a combination of both caste and class, whereby he included industrial workers, agricultural workers, women of all categories and ex-untouchables. After Dalit Panthers in the 1970s, we had writers like Kancha Ilaiah in the 1990s who used the word 'Bahujan', a term used earlier by Phule. When Kancha Ilaiah uses the term, 'Bahujan', he refers to SC, ST, OBC and minorities and amongst minorities particularly those who have converted from Hinduism to other religions like Dalit Christians, Dalit Muslims, Dalit Sikhs, Dalit Buddhists, etc. And unless and until they all come together, change is not possible. So, for a political reason, a larger unity is feasible. When we now talk about Dalit Literature, it is not just about class but a fusion of caste and class, whereby the idea of what we call 'Dalit consciousness' works. It comes from the Ambedkarite movement, Dalit Consciousness has to be a combination of both. Caste is static, class is dynamic. Once a Dalit, always a Dalit and once a Brahmin, always a Brahmin. Class can change, one can be a rich Dalit but socially will remain a Dalit nevertheless. Mayawati will always be considered as a Dalit Chief Minister. We currently have a Dalit

President. Dalit will always be a prefix. Shyamlal has written an autobiography, *Untold Story of a Bhangi Vice-Chancellor*, so even amongst higher classes, Dalit will always be prefixed.

Chawla: In March 2017, a prominent Ambedkarite, Krishna Kiravale was murdered in Kolhapur. Do you feel that his oratory skills were considered a threat in propagating the Ambedkar ideology through which more and more people were converging to the centre?

Kumar: Orality travels far and wide, and since Dalit communities all over India are not fully literate, that is why orality works. Oral literature is very rich, it attracts people's attention. For example, in Kalyan Rao's *Untouchable Spring*, the idea of orality is potent. Rao talks about, how Yellanna, the first generation of Dalit activists bring Dalit consciousness to villages through their performances. Orality is dynamic, but there is always a problem with orality as it is never documented, but at one level there is popularity, people are attracted to it, music and dance are a part of it and Dalit communities all over India are very musical. Definitely, this is a threat to the upper classes as there is mobilization. Change is slow and gradual but [I] am hopeful that there will be a difference.

17

Need to Introduce Disability Pedagogy in Mainstream Disciplines

Hemachandran Karah

Interviewed by Chandra Nisha Singh and Manjari Chaturvedi

Manjari Chaturvedi: Please tell us about your early days as a student. How did you learn English following your school education in Tamil?

Hemachandran Karah: Initially it was indeed a messy affair. Telugu and Tamil were my primary languages of thinking, playing, and breathing. While one spoke Telugu at home, the world of learning opened up solely in Tamil. This is not to mention the amount of rote learning in Tamil one has to comply with during the waking hours.

When I joined Loyola College in Madras/Chennai, I chose to read English Literature. This was in a sense taking the English language like the bull by the horns. But actually, it was not that difficult; thanks to bazaar guidebooks. I used to depend upon them heavily. Interestingly, they all had Tamil and English summaries and cursory reviews of the novels by Jane Austen, Thomas Hardy, and what not. So, one can get a feel of a novel with a detailed vernacular review. They also offered me a cultural translation of a British world which was so distant by way of language, culture, and time. Moreover,

Earlier published in *FORTELL* Issue No. 29 (July 2014).

these guidebooks are templates of our examination-driven academia. All one has to do is to commit the template contents to memory. The templates host paraphrases, theme-based answers, synonyms of difficult words and phrases, and even commentaries on the historical context of a literary masterpiece. Probably, one can claim that the bazaar guidebooks were an erstwhile Wikipedia portal in themselves. Obviously, many of us helped ourselves with many of them to crack a seemingly advanced undergraduate course in English.

On the spoken English front, my first port of call was always the BBC. Those days imitating the accent of a BBC reporter was my fond hobby! Of course, the BBC stuff did not help me with written English. My teachers, both at tertiary level and thereafter, told me that my writing was sketchy, illogical, and completely unorganized. Then, and now, we haven't evolved structures beyond a classroom setting that can cater to pupils who are in a similar situation.

In inclusive education, the main issue is not about how to make books (audio and braille) accessible, but the concern is the starting point. In an unequal marathon setting like ours, students start at different points; one who has a better cultural capital begins the race already much ahead of others, and some lag behind so much that their starting point is far behind the track area. We need to understand this first before talking about disability pedagogy. That said, I started much later for a career in writing. Writing is a different game altogether. One can deploy camouflages in the spoken domain, and not so easily in the written medium.

Chandra Nisha Singh: Are you saying that accessibility is not such an important issue?

Karah: No, not at all. I just wanted to say that college education should begin with the premise that things are not equal at the starting point. Book accessibility, for example, was a huge problem for me then. When I was at Loyola College, I used to go around in search of my readers. They generously spent a substantial part of their everyday lives in recording lessons for blind students like me.

Concerning writing, I truly became appreciative of the art of writing during my doctoral programme at Cambridge. My supervisor Dr. Tim Cribb spent a good deal of time in explaining the subtle differences between 'good word', and the almost 'good word'. A wrong idiom would trigger a discussion about English language usage across continents.

Singh: What about your school days?

Karah: It was good fun, I must say. However, all the blind schools, including mine, perform with the assumption that the sighted world outside is an ideal one. We should all aspire to integrate well in there.

Singh: Had you been in an inclusive classroom, what difference would have been there in your learning process?

Karah: For language learning three things are important. The first is the development of an appropriate lexicon. When somebody acquires knowledge basically via listening, there is a chance that he or she is forever anxious about spelling, vocabulary, and other nuances of word usage. A classic case is that of Ved Mehta, a celebrated blind autobiographer and essayist. In *All for Love* (2001), the protagonist confesses that he is shy to do touch-typing since he feels embarrassed about basic spelling mistakes. In his letter to a girlfriend, for example, he spells the word 'taxi' with 'y' at the end. Like Mehta, I often stumble upon a score of new words which are spelt very differently. My recent catch is 'Korea', which I thought is always spelt with a 'ch' in the beginning like the word 'choir'. After all, I have always heard the word Korea via several casual reading sessions with my friends. It never occurred to me to cross-check such an idiosyncratic auditory association. So, what is the lesson? For language pedagogy of the blind, braille material is a basic prerequisite. If blind children are given vocabulary training in braille, the chances are that they will get a comprehensive view concerning lexical idiosyncracies. Other disabilities obviously will require some other sets of solutions.

The second component involves communication. Developing communication competency is more than a training in fluency. Our conversations and speech improvisations for example, are accompanied by gestures, facial expressions, and a propensity to establish contact with an audience. All these communicative nuances do not occur to us automatically. They accrue usually via observation and imitation. Certain higher-level communication rhetoric is acquired only by training. These include a lawyer's tactics concerning the art of cross-examination, a sales person's perspicacity, and a doctor's concerned gaze. People with sensory disabilities miss out on communicative competence. Due to social exclusion, they rarely get an opportunity to learn by imitation and observation.

And the third component is the idiom. Proper expressions and use of right idioms are a matter of good training in writing. On this count, disabled pupils are not exclusively disadvantaged. Our centres of higher education are increasingly investing in oral performance and not good writing. If I dare say, they teach ideology, and not ways and means to think through a problem.

Concerning disability pedagogy and language learning, one may consider specific contexts of disabled students such as their reliance on 'Assistive Technologies'. To give you an example, I always had a problem with punctuation. My sentences for example, were profuse with commas. An undue proliferation of commas gave the impression that the writer-figure is twisted and shapelessly broken inside. In seeking the truth behind the problem, Tim asked me to read a few paragraphs with the aid of my screen reader. (Screen readers are special audio technologies that read aloud a computer screen). Hurrah! He discovered that my screen reader is set to read sentences with loads of pauses in between. Over a period of time, Tim reasoned, I developed a habit to mime the technology in making my sentences to read with as many pauses. It did not take much time to get out of a comma spree once I came to know about such a basic influence. A million other insights are bound to emerge once we choose to opt for a more enabling learning environment.

Singh: Do we mean that in an inclusive classroom if a teacher uses traditional methods without taking into account the specific requirements of the disabled students, these gaps would be too pronounced?

Karah: I think one can take the assistance of special educators. Besides, we can introduce disability pedagogy as an integral component in ongoing teacher-training programmes.

Chaturvedi: Is there some special training that could be given to teachers or is sensitization enough for the teachers to be able to deal with such classrooms? Are you in favour of mixing students?

Karah: I am in favour of mixing students beyond high school education.

Chaturvedi: So, in that situation, how do you think a teacher should or will be able to address different needs? Are there different needs, specifically in the Indian situation?

Karah: Sensitization is always helpful; but it can go only so far. There must be a special education person in every school who can advise about everyday problems. A deaf student. for example, requires sign language support, and also a friendly multilingual atmosphere.

Chaturvedi: Should there be some sort of language labs to address such issues? Do we have any such innovation in place in India or is it something we can create here?

Karah: So far, I reason, disability-related training courses such as a diploma in teaching the blind, diploma in deaf education, etc. target exclusive school environments. As far as I am aware, they are not integrated well with a mainstream field such as English Language Teaching (ELT). ELT is a specialized discipline. It is very different from a course in literary criticism. All four modules in ELT such as listening, speaking, reading, and writing will obviously benefit by a reflection concerning disabilities; be it cerebral, emotional, or sensory ones. Disability is not always a problem, it can be a resource too.

Chaturvedi: What sort of engagement does ELT have with disability?

Karah: It is not conspicuously there yet.

Chaturvedi: Is it something that's not begun yet? What about work in the West?

Karah: Nothing has been done systematically till now. ELT needs to do a lot of catching up work. However, the Western world can afford expensive technologies. For example, for people with dyslexia there is a software called Kurzweil 3000. It aids people with dyslexia to handle choice of words, synonyms, grammar, and an appropriate sentence structure. Fortunately, Kurzweil 3000 and the like are not beyond the reach of Indian centres of learning. However, East or West, technology is not a substitute for hard thinking about disability. A special focus in ELT concerning disability pedagogy is bound to make language accessibility a mainstream concern, and not a sideline issue.

Singh: But don't you think that this is ultimately a difficult proposition, and only possible in theory. I can visualize immense problems in its implementation. Do you think we can achieve our goal?

Karah: We probably need a two-pronged strategy. On the one hand, we have to be conscious of people with different requirements. A resource centre for example, can aid universities to produce reference materials in accessible format. The second method is to introduce disability pedagogy in mainstream disciplines themselves. Our BEd programmes can have disability pedagogy as a primary component. With no exception, Literary Studies can also include a module on special needs. I don't think we have a self-reflexive teaching module in Literary Studies. For example, it is assumed that if you have a PhD degree, you are automatically equipped to handle students who are tuned to different paces of learning. Some professors of literature simply do not know how to mentor students. Literary scholarship requires an ability to peruse reams of secondary material, close reading tactics, skimming through pages in a book, a way with words, and an acute reflective capacity. All these skills are not innate. They require rigorous, and yet empathetic literary pedagogy. In the absence of such support arrangements, disabled students will end up taking all the abuses.

Chaturvedi: Is disability a state of mind or is it a creation of society? Is there a real disparity or is it something that one just assumes, both from the point of the disabled and that of the others?

Karah: It is both. Let us take an example, imagine a blind student in a classroom situation where a teacher offers all the crucial stuff via the blackboard method. If no one were to translate things for him/her, all that is written out there will make no sense. Now, the blackboard is an essential tool for many. To make the tool relevant for a blind student too, a teacher can offer oral relays of blackboard notes, which can otherwise be nothing more than a chalk piece screech.

In Class 11, I did Accountancy, and my teacher was clearly aware of my specific requirement. He would vocalize everything that he wrote on the blackboard. He told me that the debit account is always on the left side and the credit scores are always on the right. So whenever he mentioned credit, I would automatically pull up in my mind the required mental picture. He was able to pool together certain tricks of the trade in accountancy pedagogy that renders the discipline friendly to everyone in the classroom. Similarly for every discipline such small manoeuverings can make all the difference.

Now, there is the issue of the burden of disability. Negative symbols and ideas can inculcate the notion that disability is a burdensome affair. Probably, disabled people work through them all their lives. They find it hard to cultivate a positive self-imagery inside. Writers such as Ved Mehta struggle with them all the while. On the education front, it is important to cultivate a positive imagery. However, we need to confront constraints that come with disability head on. Brilliant solutions may emerge from such a confrontation.

18

Teachers Have to be Updated in Both Technology and Knowledge

Pushpinder Syal

Interviewed by Iqbal Judge

Iqbal Judge: The internet has opened up a fascinating world of new genres of writing, for example, hyper-fiction. What are your views about it?

Pushpinder Syal: The hyper-text offers these choices of links to readers, who have the feeling of interacting with the text, in a way making up their own story as they go along. But that is very much the case in other kinds of reading also, except that neither does the reader feel that he/she is doing that explicitly, nor is it explicitly encoded in the text as such. In reading a traditional novel, the reader is in fact doing the same things, is following the text in continuity, and at the same time carrying on a simultaneous process in his/her own mind, except that the reader does not in a meta-activity kind of thing, think about what he/she is doing.

Judge: There is a mental conversation going on with the text, 'what is this about', and there is a physical engagement also, because you make a choice and click a particular link.

Syal: Yes, re-reading, backtracking, or taking divergent paths. Geoffrey Leech in *Style in Fiction* talks about the 'garden path phenomenon', which makes you think that 'Oh, this is what

---

Earlier published in *FORTELL* Issue No. 33 (July 2016).

the writer is saying', but actually they're leading to something else, in their very structure. So, there are hundreds of such micro-decisions that the reader is making all along and I would guess that the people who make these hyper-texts are probably stylisticians in this way. They have latched on to what readers do while engaging with a text, and capitalized on that by offering the reader these choices and I suppose it has an advantage in that readers do become more conscious.

But when it comes to more complex things, to writing, that is the preservation of memory of a particular ethos or a historical period, where the aim is preservation of memory, now that kind of activity, I don't think anything can replace extended, discursive writing because it so subjective, so personal, and evoking an entire culture, a way of life, so I feel that these two types of writing inhabit different spheres.

Judge: Do you think these writings would be more in the detective fiction genre? Some of the texts/passages are also quite brief, the links as well, sometimes just a few sentences.

Syal: Yes, I suppose so. It probably does lend itself to this kind of mystery or whodunit kind of structure.

Judge: Would they be useful in pedagogy?

Syal: Certainly, because it's not just stories, it's also following a train of thought, a lot of logical thinking, theorizing, making predictions. For example, 'Do you think it happens this way? Can it happen this way or that way?' You give choices to the learner, and the learner can explore those choices further to their possible limits. My feeling is that there is tremendous potential, something that learners would surely enjoy, and perhaps it would be better than doing a pen and paper sort of exercise, a kind of heuristic system where you're problem-solving as you go along, in a very explicit manner. There could also be links in this system, where you could be asked to talk to your friend about a certain topic or issue and with that kind of outreach, it could become even more interactive, open out to even more discussions with others, making the learners feel that they are actually 'doing' something.

Judge: Something like in our traditional post-reading activity, a different take-off point say like prediction or evaluative exercises, project-work, reading beyond the textbook?

Syal: Yes, exactly! In the hyper-text, you have even more possibilities: it could be ongoing, the text could keep changing all the time, and the exercises could be inbuilt.

It's also a question of different registers. Some of the registers are a greater mix of speech and writing. In text messaging for example, all kinds of abbreviations, emoticons, etc., are allowed; it's a cross between speech and writing, trying to overcome the shortcomings of each mode, since the technology is now available for doing so.

Judge: That brings me to the problem which teachers are often plagued with, that text messaging is ruining students' language, writing skills, that they seem to be writing, but it's actually not writing.

Syal: Yes, because it is actually not writing but a mix of speech and writing and of course it's popular, that's why the fear that it will replace other modes! But it's not going to destroy other registers; they are coexisting and will continue to coexist; the registers are expanding all the time.

If one's writing ability is only limited to text messaging, then that would probably be a limitation in your education, in the way you're going to get knowledge and convey knowledge, because you couldn't stretch it very far, where you need to contribute to a discussion in a sustained way, and need much more ability than just the ability to send across messages.

Judge: So it would be important to make students aware of different registers and styles, especially as teachers now are worried, 'Oh now they're only using emoticons, they don't have the vocabulary to express what they feel, because the emoticon does it for them.'

Syal: In the classroom it could be quite a lot of fun to translate from one register into another. Give them a long-winded structure and say, shorten it to an emoticon.

Judge: Or the other way around, 'What adjectives would best express the given emoticon?' Or give a very terse, enigmatic kind of text message, 'Expand it', to see if they get the same message out of it.

Syal: But again we've got to remember that any activity will be taken up if it is seen as meaningful, and in a context. If we just give them a text message to expand into a paragraph, it would quickly seem to be too much of a dull academic exercise, so the same problem remains: how do we contextualize some of these activities, how do we make them meaningful? Let's go back again to our hyper-fiction: if at a particular point, a particular message had to be conveyed, then, 'What option would you choose', or something like that; activities built into a larger story- telling framework. Educational frameworks do need to have something extra in them, a value addition: there is a VAT in pedagogy as well! Something that is not in the framework of our experience, which we do need to know.

Judge: The latest buzz word is the flipped classroom. I wonder if that isn't just old wine in new bottles. Is it just because we're thinking of the attraction of the internet, that students will have read the text, because it's online or because there's a video attached to it?

Syal: Not necessarily, because there are hundreds of other fascinating things online as well to distract them from their tasks. So, I think the basic question is: where does the teacher's input really lie? If they have read the text, the teacher may raise some issues, and then give an assignment or ask the students to do an activity and so on. Now that is an issue for the teacher, because I've often found that however much I might want to throw the thing open, even if they've read and come (first of all that itself is a tall order, because even if it is a poem to read online, it still is a reading task, so you are assuming a certain level of proficiency in English), you find yourself imposing a particular perspective, and the students get a cue from that, and they realize what direction to go in, so willy-nilly the teacher is giving a direction, giving some input.

Judge: And needs to, perhaps.

Syal: And needs to, yes. So what kind of ability does it demand of the teacher? What kind of subjectivity does the teacher bring to the class? The teacher may be opinionated, or biased; a lot depends on how clever and successful he/she is in making the students produce a particular kind of response. Are we sure about what kind of input we need to give to the students? Or is it that in a technology-driven classroom, the teacher is just an instructor, directing the students—go to this link, find this and that, and the students keep busy, clicking links, downloading, etc., though that might be useful also, because for many people in societies that are new to technology sifting through the jungle of information available can be very off-putting. So perhaps one of the roles of the teacher would be to navigate through the mass of information, point out places of interest, which could be tapped as you move along, but that means the teacher has to be updated in terms of both technology and knowledge.

Judge: Yes, the teacher can give pointers, for example, grammar exercises on the internet are much more interactive, and self-motivating because you submit your answer, you immediately get to know what is the right answer, or where and why you were wrong. It also saves the teacher the bother of repetitively checking numerous such assignments.

Syal: Sure, but that's not your physical classroom and that's like self-learning; there the teacher is the facilitator. There would also be several teachers who make the programme that is going to auto-correct the exercises, someone working behind the scenes, and increasingly we find many of our linguistically proficient students getting placements in software companies as content writers for these programmes.

Even in our tech-enabled classroom, where the learners are busy working at their tasks, they may have questions, want more exercises or clarifications, so that's where the teacher might have to intervene, go back to the explanatory mode, even go back to the blackboard to illustrate certain concepts, explain a structure that many of the students have not been able to get right. So, the teacher would have to be ready to anticipate problems, give examples, etc. because no software can be complete in that respect. I suspect that one of the reasons for resistance to the technology-enabled classroom is that it's going to be a challenge in terms of the technology itself, in understanding how the programme works.

Judge: What if they are going to make the programmes themselves?

Syal: To a great extent they will have to, because no programme can ever fit all sizes. A lot of it will have to be localized; there is very little material that can be standardized to such an extent that everyone everywhere can use it. It's not just a question of culture-specific content or something like that, it's a concern of more specific questions that some learners would be asking, and we can't always anticipate them. So the challenge is huge. The teacher needs to have a fiar amount of computer literacy to use the web tools available; also collaboration with makers of programmes, so that teachers can guide them to critically monitor the ideology that underlies them; not just being the end-receivers of that technology, but creating that kind of technology.

We also have to consider how equally tech becomes available to all, and not just available to the privileged. It becomes an extension of the print culture then, where it created an elite that could afford books.

Judge: What about mobile phone apps, online dictionaries, or learning apps, such as 'Hello English'? Do you think they are empowering the learner?

Syal: Yes, but look at what it presupposes—motivation; and that again remains one of the fundamental questions. Whether it is the flipped classroom or the mobile app, the fundamental human questions remain the same: 'What am I as a teacher going to give?' And for the learner, 'What motivates me to learn? Shall I open this app and learn those five words of the day or not?'

We say that the big motivation in English is jobs, but is everything job-oriented, or is it something the person wants to be, some quality of life that the learner is looking for? We have the experience of the call centres, where ultimately people were not happy, so these are broader human questions: 'Does the person simply operate language as a machine, or use it as a self-enhancing medium?' There's a crucial difference between simply operating a technology and knowing that there is a particular kind of ideology operating behind the programme as well, being able to come to that critical point of understanding, which is important both for the teacher and the learner.

19

Role of the Teacher is No Longer the 'Sage on the Stage', But the 'Guide on the Side'

Pete Sharma

Interviewed by Sabina Pillai

Sabina Pillai: You have stated that you wear many hats. Can you please elucidate for our readership in India?

Pete Sharma: The hats represent different roles I have enjoyed in my professional career. The first so-called hat is of course a teaching hat. I have taught Business English, mostly in Spain and Finland, but also in the Middle East and Far East. Nowadays I lecture in EAP, that is English for Academic Purposes.

My second hat as a teacher trainer has provided many challenges [such as] trying to understand which beliefs and attitudes inform an individual teacher's practice.

I am now well established as an author, my third hat, and yet I never intended to be a writer. I always describe myself as an accidental author. I wanted a book on CD-ROM so badly that I ended up writing one myself! Thanks to Summertown Publishing for giving me that opportunity.

My fourth and final hat is [that of a] a reviewer. I write the 'Reviews in Brief' column for the Bournemouth English Book Centre, which appears in the *EL Gazette*, the international

---

Earlier published in *FORTELL* Issue No. 38 (January 2019).

journal for EFL (English as a Foreign Language) teachers. I have loved receiving hundreds of review books over the years and can now claim one of the largest individual libraries around! One result of wearing so many hats is that you end up seeing things from many different perspectives like management, sales and teaching.

Pillai: What are your current areas of interest in these fields?

Sharma: My current areas of interest lie within the field of TELL—technology-enhanced language learning. They are AR (augmented reality) and VR (virtual reality). AR involves overlaying digital information onto the real world, usually through apps; VR is an immersive 360 degree experience usually involving putting on a headset. I also have a great interest in M-learning—mobile learning—and love my Smartphone and iPad. Obviously, the area of blended learning fascinates me, as does the area of vocabulary review.

Pillai: You have a special interest in using technology in language teaching and many of the books you have authored/co-authored are in this area. Could you please tell us more?

Sharma: The first time I saw a dictionary on CD-ROM, I was bitten by the technology bug. I saw how digital changed the way we can access content compared with analogue. This was very surprising for a graduate in English literature. I now wish I had been more attentive in school in Mathematics and Sciences.

The area I'm particularly interested in is the interface of technology and pedagogy. I have certainly enjoyed writing about technology in teaching over the years. My second teacher development book in this area, *The Internet and Business English*, co-written with long-term friend and colleague Barney Barrett, was 'Highly Commended' in the Duke of Edinburgh ESU awards. It was a great day, collecting the certificate from Buckingham Palace. My third book, *Learning: Using Technology in and Beyond the Language Classroom* (Macmillan), was shortlisted for the Ben Warren International House Trust prize. Two of my recent publications are E-books—on apps and writing digital materials.

Pillai: How would you define blended learning in ELT? Please tell us more about your new book.

Sharma: Blended learning is a combination of traditional face-to-face classroom teaching and web-based learning. It means different things to different people and has multiple definitions. For example, there is a new term, 'virtual blend', so the face-to-face part of a course is not done in a traditional classroom but online. The complete term is 'face-to-face online' such as a Skype call. It can be slightly confusing!

My latest book is a comprehensive, practical handbook which explores the whole area of blended learning. The book provides definitions of BL, a brief history of the term and an exploration of what the research says. It looks at the reasons why schools and teachers decide to blend and the challenges they face; lists the key elements for success and presents a practical framework for designing a BL course. It gives an overview of some of the many learning platforms available. The book is full of practical ideas.

We are so fortunate that the book includes case studies from around the world, including Venezuela and Tunisia. The online support includes guides on building your own platform and creating digital materials. Having done this interview for *FORTELL*, I'm hoping that a teacher might offer a case from India.

Pillai: There is a great deal of talk about the emerging potential of using technology through mobile learning, AR (augmented reality) and VR (virtual reality). Do you think such current or imminent trends in language teaching will bring about better learning outcomes?

Sharma: In many ways, this is the $64,000 question: 'will they bring about "better learning outcomes"?'

Nicky Hockly, a well-known author in the field, asks the question: 'Do digital technologies support language learning?'

Hockly concludes 'the jury is still out', as the effectiveness (or lack of effectiveness) of a particular technology depends on a wide range of factors, such as how it is used. Measuring learning outcomes is notoriously difficult.

That's the research perspective. However, a common sense perspective says that if you can learn anywhere, anytime, and if you can be in control of the exposure you get to the language being learnt, and if such learning through AR and VR motivates, then surely it's a better time to learn languages than in the pre-digital era. That's what I believe.

Pillai: Is blended learning superior to the traditional methods of teaching and learning? How would we address issues of access, infrastructure and expertise in non-elite environments?

Sharma: Is blended learning superior? Rather than 'BL is superior', I prefer to rephrase the question as: 'Does BL have the potential to be effective?' It's about harnessing the best elements of classroom learning (like a great teacher) with the best elements of online (like studying when and where you like and not just when the timetable demands) and working towards a math equation: 1 + 1 is more than 2. It could be better, but equally it could fail as it merely bolts together two modes—face-to-face plus online—without any underlying pedagogical principles.

We should always be cautious on hearing phrases like 'superior' or 'the best method' because there cannot really be one method which is better than all others. Language learners are different and what makes one student tick may not affect another.

Access, infrastructure and expertise are complex issues. Access is often limited and yet some of the most creative and innovative teaching and learning is done in difficult circumstances, like in refugee camps and no-tech contexts. I know so little about the local context of most learners in India for example, despite a few visits to the subcontinent (where I was born by the way) and would love to learn more. One thing is clear—expertise. India has a high level of expertise in technology. However, I believe there may be many instances of outdated, teacher-centred approaches. There certainly were when I visited Bangladesh. Rote-chanting due to large classes for example. I cannot be prescriptive, as an outsider to the local context, but the world of educational technologies is fast-moving and it makes sense to strive to keep up with it.

Pillai: Would technology in the classroom displace the importance of the teacher? What would happen to the agency of the teacher? Her motivation to excel as a teacher?

Sharma: Teaching is not only about teaching well. It is about creating optimum conditions for language learning. Most teachers know their role is no longer the 'sage on the stage', but the 'guide on the side'. If a teacher has the students' interests as central, they should have no real problems fearing for their importance. Students need help and guidance in navigating the internet and using the raft of tools at their disposal. Excellent teaching provides for excellent learning, and unlocking potential.

Pillai: Would such technology prove to be intimidating for the average teacher? How different is it from mainstream technology? Would it become burdensome for a teacher to be computer savvy to be able to operate a programme written by a third party?

Sharma: Many aspects of using technology may at first sight prove intimidating for a language teacher. However, with a little bit of effort, most obstacles fall away as much of technology has become increasingly user-friendly. You can usually work out how to use an iPad intuitively. There are many crossovers between mainstream technologies and educational technology. We often feel comfortable using tech in our lives—sending emails and using smartphones. It's a small step into the classroom. Let us not forget Sugata Mitra and his 'Hole in the Wall' project where Indian children taught themselves how to use a computer. Many fears in the area are, if we're being honest, more to do with the fact that children know more about (say) Snapchat than the teachers. The children might not know the term 'augmented reality', but when they superimpose a dinosaur onto a scene in Snapchat, that's what they're using! So no, it's not too onerous to learn enough to operate successfully in our profession.

Pillai: Would such technology-based learning, which perforce is objective by nature, dehumanize learning and deprive it of all the ideology that underlines it?

Sharma: Yes, this is a possible danger and some might argue that this kind of 'dehumanization' already happens to some extent. Learning systems gather data with a view to determine learning paths and personalize learning. Translation tools help, allowing two people who do speak each other's language to communicate, but with an absence of cultural understanding. It is up to us in teaching to be critical of developments like AI (artificial intelligence) and RALL (robot-assisted language learning), and sceptical of pedagogically unsound developments in technology. If students practise chatting with a robot, the overall aim is to communicate with people in real life.

Pillai: How would we overcome the 'one size does not fit all' syndrome, when using standardized technology-based lessons? Is digital technology an effective tool for students of all abilities? Does digital technology help accommodate students' personal learning styles?

Sharma: I agree one size does not fit all. There should not necessarily be a standardized technology lesson. I give my students a choice of which way they would like to review their new words—maybe in an analogue way with a Vocabulary Notebook, (yes! I co-wrote the Vocabulary Notebook) or by using one of many apps, Quizlet, Anki, Memrise.

Technology can really help provide differentiation, with students choosing their own pathways through the material, choosing how many times to listen to a video, whether to access subtitles or not.

With the teachers' help, technology can really help students by allowing them to identify their own personal learning styles. The teacher can steer them towards good practice through strategy training.

Pillai: How do you perceive educational technology synergizing with ELT in the classroom? Do digital technologies support language learning? How do teachers use digital technology for assessment? Does it make it easier or more cumbersome?

Sharma: There are many tech tools which can be used appropriately in class, learner response systems, for example. Similarly, there are many tools best used between lessons, such as speak-to-text apps and much of technology can be used inside or outside the classroom. As Jones wrote many years ago, 'it's not so much the program, more what you do with it'. There's no doubt in my mind that many digital technologies support language learning. Who wants to ditch the word processor (which helps re-draft writing) and return to the age of the typewriter? Having said that, we must remain with our pedagogical feet firmly on the ground and not get carried away with the grander claims of what big data, artificial intelligence and other developments can 'do for you'.

Regarding assessment, digital technology has really made a huge difference. It is far easier and quicker to use a computer-based placement test. Adaptive learning has improved such tests enormously. A low-level student does not have to sit in silence till the end of the test as they did in previous, one-size fits all testing. Rather, they are accurately placed by the computer's ability to generate the next, appropriate question based on the student's previous answer. However, we must remember that language learning has a humanistic side which is hard to measure, and includes a free-speaking element which involves confidence, eye contact and para-linguistic features, not easily assessable by a machine.

Pillai: What would be the implications for ELT pedagogy in the classroom as there would be less teaching and more of facilitating by the teacher? Could digital technology reduce the number of teachers employed in the future?

Sharma: It was once said that 'Any teacher who is replaced by a computer, deserves to be!' We know that automation is here to stay; that robots will 'rise' and many repetitive jobs will disappear. Teachers should get busy being creative. Technology is less unlikely to replace the creative teacher. Teachers and technology working hand-in-glove? Now yes, that's a different story. Voice-recognition bots and Amazon's Alexa can be involved in exchanges with learners, but they do not replace the creative teacher. Even the robots helping classes in Korea are only able to deal with predictable interchanges, and not the infinite variety of responses which the human mind is capable of.

Pillai: How does technology deliver quality in education? Would audio-visual content enhance learning or distract the learner?

Sharma: Technology can enhance the teaching and learning which takes place on a good, quality course. It can provide a robust, reliable learning platform for the housing of digital material. It allows distance learning through the delivery of webinars, and tools which can be used in providing online lessons. Apps can also encourage autonomous learning. Much of publisher-produced digital content may include superb graphics and video and crystal clear audio recordings, but evaluation includes not only the materials themselves but how they are used. For example, poorly shot amateur footage on YouTube taken of an exciting incident can lead to great fluency practice.

Whether or not audio-visual material is a distraction is an interesting issue. Designers should ensure that in publisher-produced material, there are few distractions for the learner following their path within digital material. Learners now need to develop new digital literacies and have to learn how to deal with hyperlinks on a web-page, and how to manage the multi-modalities on offer when navigating digital materials.

Pillai: What are the main challenges to developing digital content for ELT?

Sharma: There are many challenges for developing digital content. When you write an interactive exercise for a publisher, you envisage an idealized situation, such as a typical intermediate group. Unfortunately, such a group doesn't exist. Hence the materials may not be deemed valid by local teachers, who may prefer to develop materials themselves suited to their local context, whether that is in Riyadh, Rio, Shanghai or Bangaluru.

Much of the development of digital content nowadays involves the use of algorithms to generate responses from the software, or ASR (automated speech recognition), both of which are usually viewed negatively by sentient teachers who may see their role as being usurped by an inferior pedagogue—the software as the tutor. Digital developers are good at design, but may never have taught a language lesson and one of the main challenges of creating digital content is creating pedagogically valid material.

Pillai: Are there any downsides to the digital wave in ELT? If so, how do we tackle them?

Sharma: There are many downsides. One is cyber-bullying. Another is plagiarism. Health issues are connected with using a VR headset, currently due to latency or delay as the software is running too slowly. The above-mentioned trend in AI may generate many benefits, but currently it suffers from being at an experimental phase and viewed (rightly) with suspicion by many language teachers. The rise of fake news is another unwelcome trend.

There are many things we can do. One is to encourage our students to adhere to good online etiquette, to help them understand the deeper concept of plagiarism, which can be difficult in certain cultures, and to develop critical thinking skills. Clearly, the role of the teacher has changed from just being a language teacher, to steering our young learners towards global citizenship and developing their digital literacies so they can fully participate in this new, exciting but daunting technological world.

20

Quality and Integrity are Essential Features of Distance Learning

Richard Allen

Interviewed by Ruchi Kaushik

Ruchi Kaushik: Distance learning in Higher Education (HE) has been garnering a lot of interest in the last few years, be it in government or university policies or general learner attitude. According to you, what are the main reasons for this shift?

Richard Allen: It's tempting to be somewhat cynical here and say that distance education is interesting to those in government or in university management because it offers ways of expanding Higher Education (HE) provision without a proportionate increase in fixed costs involved in buildings, etc. But I think the majority of distance education initiatives have had a strong moral purpose, the desire particularly to reach students in social, economic and geographic groups who are under-represented in HE. I think it's also possible that the methods of teaching associated with distance education are now perceived to be better, so are more interesting to those interested in teaching and learning. This is particularly the case where it is possible to build systems on the basis of new technology. In a number of countries in the past distance education was identified with poor quality (in all senses of the

---

Earlier published in *FORTELL* Issue No. 30 (January 2015).

phrase) photocopied materials sent out by post. Students were expected passively to absorb these materials and there was minimal interactivity and limited support. Learning based on computing and communication technology regularly supersedes that approach, enabling students studying at home to actually feel closer to their teachers than a student studying ostensibly 'face-to-face' (but actually usually only 'glimpsed at a distance') on a large campus. New technology also provides far more effective and far more secure possibilities for assessment. The important thing here is that teachers need to be trained and resourced to use distance learning, primarily to benefit students but also to overcome the prejudice against distance learning which is entwined with the lack of interest you mention.

Kaushik: Off-campus learning is often perceived to be similar to other modes of education such as *online learning, e-learning, blended learning, open-learning, life-long learning,* etc. All these apparently have a lot in common and yet are dissimilar in many ways. Could you briefly explain the main features of off-campus learning?

Allen: You're right that there are a number of terms which are used in ways that suggest each is separate but in practice that's not the case. I could begin by saying that I can't now imagine *blended learning* that didn't involve *e-learning*. *E-learning* is most often imagined as *online learning* but might also be on-campus *computer-room learning*. When *blended learning* features *online e-learning* it is often because it is *open-learning* or *life-long learning*. It should be obvious from this that what is at issue is *education*. The main features of good off-campus learning are then the same as the main features of good on-campus learning. Off-campus learning can be done badly, just as on-campus learning can be done badly, but the faults are more damaging for students because they tend to be studying on their own and can easily become disheartened.

So the main systemic features of off-campus learning have

to be quality and integrity. Particularly given the prejudice against distance education, off-campus education has to aim to be the best, to the point that on-campus teachers want to borrow from off-campus. Beyond that you need a system which has been thought through. Whether you are dealing with off-campus learning that leads to a whole degree or smaller units of learning to provide updating professional or technical skills you need an effective registration system with secure assessment. Quality teaching is a must, but that needs to be articulated with good resources for learning. At the Open University (OU), for example, we've created virtual field trips for environmental studies, and virtual libraries for the Humanities. Good management of the processes for course design are important, and since the use of technology seems almost inevitable you also need specialist support there—for students, teachers and course development.

Kaushik: Well, talking of Open University (OU), UK, it is one of the pioneer institutions in distance learning established in 1969 and your association with it dates back to several decades. Can you please tell us about the objectives behind establishment of the Open University and whether it has succeeded in fulfilling them?

Allen: The original (and I think continuing) objectives of the OU are embodied in the two words of its title; we seek to be open in a whole range of ways, and to be a university in the fullest possible sense. We often link the idea of 'openness' to opportunities; we make opportunities for HE study available to people who are housebound or serving in a submarine, or who just want to study with us to improve their skills and qualifications. We aim to make the opportunities for study that we provide challenging and engaging to encourage students to keep studying. We also ensure that our standards of assessment are unchallenged through systems which use external examiners beyond the norm in UK education.

Perhaps the most distinctive feature of our openness is

that at undergraduate level we set no entry requirements. We have comprehensive advice systems so that students aren't recruited who will immediately fail and drop out, but beyond that students make their own decisions about entry and we do everything we can to support their aspirations. Of course, the situation has changed drastically since when we registered our first students. The OU has also increased its ambitions especially in terms of geographical reach and the use of technology. Most recently it has established Future Learn in which a wide range of other universities join with the OU to provide MOOCs (Massive Open Online Courses). So students began with books, television and radio, and moved onto video cassettes, DVDs and the internet, things are changing all the time.

As for objectives being achieved, they are dynamic and changing but more or less we have been successful. Overall we challenge ourselves as we encourage our students to challenge themselves; we have the same kind of intellectual and social aspirations now as we did at the beginning but have adapted to fit the changing world order. The support we gave to IGNOU, the Singapore Institute of Management, and the Arab Open University signal the breadth of our aims. The English Department interestingly played a major part in these latter two schemes; students wanted to study English as well as management just as they do in India. We want to be the best; it is difficult to find another institution which combines the same range of excellences—in teaching, research and development of new educational technologies.

Kaushik: The support and collaboration among Open Universities across the world is certainly an important feature of this dynamic field. Distance learning is a rapidly evolving area of education. Can you please elaborate some prerequisites for ensuring quality distance education in the Indian context?

Allen: I think three things are key to the development of distance learning. First, distance learning should be quality learning. Second is the understanding that good learning here must involve student activity and interactivity just as much as in face-to-face on campus teaching. Third, the development of technology must enable real interactivity; for example, Moodle has empowered teachers to create their own materials rather than having somehow to fit it into some complex prescribed programme that only the IT people understand.

If I think about these three things in relation to the evolution of distance learning in India, I want to say first that the pursuit of quality and standards has to be absolute: that would involve securing accreditation and endorsement of quality to a degree. Equally distance learning has to be interactive to be effective, and that means a sea change in the way teachers and students work, setting aside the old system of rote learning. One of the key inventions here at the Open University has been the role of the part-time tutor. This is someone who takes responsibility for a group of twenty or so students and for the facilitation of the learning devised by the central faculty. Students rely on part-time tutors to help them solve problems in their learning and also in their lives (meeting deadlines, etc.) Where I pause is on the issue of technology; in the cities maybe technology will be important, but in the countryside where education is so much needed, it needs people to think things through differently. But maybe things aren't so different from the way they were here in the UK in the earlier days where people depended on telephone contact with their tutor to keep going and achieve success.

Kaushik: The common perception in India about distance education is that the course and the degree offered via the distance mode are inferior to the conventional course and degree both in terms of content and market value. What is your take on this?

Allen: As I have mentioned earlier, it is essential to have strong, transparent and publicly recognized Quality Assurance processes to ensure proper standards. That might be easier in an organization dedicated to distance learning like the OU or IGNOU. It's perhaps harder to establish distinct QA processes for distance education where that is just an adjunct to a large face-to-face teaching system. Processes have also to be owned throughout the organization, so that those teaching distance programmes are insistent on Quality Assurance, that way, they get the respect of their students and employers. Distance teaching is often more publicly visible than face-to-face teaching; books are published and websites are open to scrutiny, whereas what goes on in a lecture hall is often known only to the teacher and the students. That means again that those involved in distance teaching need to be ambitious and strive for the best.

Kaushik: You are right; there can be no short cuts in quality Assurance to give distance education the desired respectability. But do you think that as an educational mode it functions better for some subjects, say Social Sciences and Humanities than Sciences?

Allen: I think distance teaching is suited to all disciplines so long as those involved are prepared to make an effort into working out how technology can help. We've always taught science subjects at the OU. Initially we sent out kits of materials so that students could do experiments at home, guided by printed instructions and television programmes. Now we've moved on to using virtual reality and other high-tech systems to achieve the same ends. Archive resources can be made available in a closed 'library' structure for History students or project work can be set up using open web resources. And of course, these techniques can be used by students working in a computer lab on a campus just as easily as they can be by those working at a distance.

Kaushik: What do you have to say about its suitability for English Studies?

Allen: The situation in English is similar. In English we began with specially produced books that were only available within the university but our skill in curriculum design and pedagogy led to our materials being taken up by publishers—I'm thinking here of the *Approaching Literature* and *The Nineteenth Century Novel* series both published by Routledge—and thus made more widely available. But now technology can be used in a whole range of ways to create hyperlinked editions of texts, computer-based assistants for language learning, techniques for enabling students to understand metre in poetry or plot structure in a novel. At the OU we've also used conferencing techniques for Creative Writing Workshops, and in fact the communications aspect of ICT is perhaps as important as anything here. Students can get together in a conference or a forum to discuss a text, helping each other (or being helped by a facilitator) at basic levels to achieve understanding of difficult materials, but also going on to understand how different meanings can interact in often unstable texts. There are lessons to be learned even from the kind of hyperlinked annotation I've mentioned; does a reading of *The Waste Land*, for example, depend on following up every reference fully, or do you need some other more dynamic model? More broadly here you can see that in English and in other subjects students learn in ways that will much more replicate the way they will need to learn after graduation; learning in groups as well as on their own, and learning from online resources rather by rote.

Kaushik: In learning through new models, technology is an important interface and that brings in its own set of problems that critics of distance education highlight. How do you think these challenges can be addressed?

Allen: There is a risk of fault on both sides here. Those who criticize distance learning in the way you suggest have often a hidden hostility to distance learning. But equally on the distance learning side there is a risk that the use of new technology and computer-based open educational resources is fetished. Really it needs people to think the situation through from a pedagogic point of view; to work out the learning outcomes that they want students to achieve and how students will learn and be assessed.

Kaushik: We are witnessing greater availability of online courses and the possibility of pursuing courses where geographical location of the learner is not a concern. Do you think in future fewer students will opt for traditional on-campus courses and a large part of their education will comprise online and off-campus courses?

Allen: I rather suspect that won't be the case, since notwithstanding the centrality of social media to younger people's lives, the pull of the social life that is part of a campus system is strong. The idea of social media is perhaps helpful here. We're not gong to be talking about a teacher-learner relation but of learners within a network comprising other learners, a tutor, and the central faculty. A student who is stuck on the meaning of a particular speech in a Shakespeare play can ask the whole community for help with students learning from each other under the corrective eye of an expert. I do think that the techniques used in distance teaching will become more common on campuses, and oddly this might be an important factor in raising the reputation of distance teaching so that they do become truly complementary.

Interviewees

Rama Kant Agnihotri, DPhil (York, UK), retired as Professor and Head, Department of Linguistics, University of Delhi. He has taught and written extensively about General Linguistics, Applied Linguistics, Morphology and Sociolinguistics.

He co-edits with A.L. Khanna *Language and Language Teaching* journal (Azim Premji University and Vidya Bhawan Society) and *Sage* series on Research in Applied Linguistics (RAL). Besides these, he has published/co-edited several books including *Crisis of Identity: A Sociolinguistic Study of Sikh Children in Leeds* (Bahri, Delhi, 1987), *Hindi: An Essential Grammar* (Routledge, London, 2007), *Hindi Morphology: A Word-based Description* (Motilal Banarsidass, Delhi, 1997, with Rajendra Singh), *Adult ESOL Learners in Great Britain* (Multilingual Matters, UK, 1998, with A.L. Khanna, M.K. Verma and S.K. Sinha), *Noam Chomsky: The Architecture of Language* (Oxford, Delhi, 2001, ed. with N. Mukherjee and B.N. Patnaik), *Indian English: Towards a New Paradigm* (Orient BlackSwan, Delhi, 2012, ed. with Rajendra Singh), *'Impure Languages': Linguistic and Literary Hybridity in Contemporary Cultures* (Orient BlackSwan, Delhi, 2012, ed. with C. Benthien and T. Oransakia), and *Trends in Language Teaching* (Orient BlackSwan, Delhi, 2017, ed. with Anju Sahgal Gupta and A.L. Khanna).

Richard Allen is Emeritus Professor in English, Faculty of Arts and Social Sciences, and Creative Writing at The Open University (OU), UK. His long career at OU has involved various leadership roles. As Dean, Faculty of Arts, he was able to expand the Faculty and its profile of courses, fostering the introduction of online teaching and also the introduction of a Creative Writing programme. Allen was a member of the Steering Group for the Quality Assurance Agency Institutional Audit in 2004, and was academic lead for the Audit in 2009, and academic lead for the reaccreditation in 2010.

Allen has been involved for a number of years in collaborative work in Indian Higher education. He has been Visiting Professor in the Departments of English at the University of Mumbai and University of Delhi. In 2004 he co-taught an MPhil class on 'Representations of India in British Writings' at DU and in 2005 acted as a consultant to the School of Open Learning there. With Savita Datta of the University of Delhi, Allen led a project funded as part of the UK India Education Initiative designed to develop capacity in the use of new technology in teaching at the University of Delhi.

Saugata Bhaduri is Professor at the Centre for English Studies, Jawaharlal Nehru University, New Delhi. His areas of interest include contemporary literary theory, popular culture studies, and translation and comparative literature studies, in all of which he has published, taught and conducted research extensively. Widely travelled, he has been a recipient of several international grants and visiting professorships from different universities and academic bodies of the UK, the Americas, and the European Union.

His major publications include *Polycoloniality* (Bloomsbury, 2019, forthcoming), *Transcultural Negotiations of Gender: Studies in (Be)Longing* (Springer, 2015, ed. with Indrani Mukherjee), *Literary Theory: An Introductory Reader* (Anthem Press, 2010, ed. with Simi Malhotra), *Perspectives on Comparative Literature and Culture in the Age of Globalization* (Anthem Press, 2010, ed. with Amar Basu), *Translating Power* (ed., Katha, 2008), and *Negotiating 'Glocalization': Views from Language Literature and Culture Studies* (ed., Anthem Press, 2008).

Rimli Bhattacharya has trained in Comparative Literature at Jadavpur and Brown Universities and works in several Indian languages as well as Russian, French and Chinese. Her primary research area includes gender and performance, primary education and children's literature. She has taught at Jadavpur University, Jawaharlal Nehru University, MS University of Baroda and has been the Rama Watumull Distinguished Indian Scholar at the University of Hawai'i at Manoa; ICCR Visiting Chair at the University of Pennsylvania; and Visiting Professor, Gender Studies, at the Centre for Studies in Social Sciences, Calcutta. She currently teaches at the Department of English, University of Delhi.

She is the author of *Binodini Dasi: 'My Story' and 'My Life as an Actress'* (1998), which includes translations of the nineteenth century actress's autobiographies. She has co-authored a book on the teaching of English in government schools, *Sur Pippa: 'Notes on Running Feet'* (2012). Her most recent book on gender and performance is *Public Women in British India: Icons on the Urban Stage* (Routledge, 2018).

Her translations from Bangla into English include short stories, autobiographies, critical essays and classics novels. Her forthcoming works include *The Dancing Poet: Rabindranath Tagore and Choreographies of Participation* (Tulika Books) and *Children's Literature in India: Many Tongues, Many Realities* (Bloomsbury Publishing).

Rod Bolitho is a freelance ELT trainer and consultant. He has worked in both state and private sectors in the UK and abroad, and from 2007-15 was Academic Director at NILE (Norwich Institute of Language Education). He has directed and taught Masters programmes at NILE and in Plymouth, and is currently lead consultant to the ELT Reform Project for the British Council in Uzbekistan.

He has visited India frequently over a period of more than 35 years and has contributed to a number of educational projects and initiatives, including the CBSE reform project, and the CPD Think Tank for the British Council. He has written articles and chapters in a number of journals and edited collections, and has co-authored books, including *Discover English* (with Brian Tomlinson), *Trainer Development* (with Tony Wright), *Continuing Professional Development* (with Amol Padwad), and *The Internationalisation of Ukrainian Universities* (with Richard West). He is currently working with Richard Rossner on *Language Education in a Changing World: Challenges and Opportunities*, for publication in 2020. Rod enjoys walking, cooking, gardening and reading and is a lifelong Liverpool FC supporter.

Dee Broughton is an English language teacher, teacher-trainer, and specialist in designing educational materials and curricula and in teaching academic research writing in developing educational systems.

Her teaching assignments include teaching academic writing to first year and international graduate students at the University of Idaho. In 2012 and 2013, she was a Senior Fellow with the US Department of State's English Language Fellow Program in Vallabh Vidyanagar, Gujarat, India where she worked with hundreds of primary, secondary, and university teachers. In India, she published several textbooks, including *Bridges: Activities for Thinking, Speaking, and Writing English*. With *Bridges*, she introduced a new design called StudyDo, and it has been adopted by a national English programme for teens in Sri Lanka. After the EL Fellowship, she returned to India as an English Language Specialist in teacher training, academic and research writing, and materials and curriculum development, and finished a second StudyDo book, *Bridges to Academic Writing*.

She has been an editor at DOAJ and is member of COPE. Through these, Dee has worked with international scholars and open-access journals to promote international standards of academic integrity. Currently, she is finishing up a new StudyDo book for B2 level academic writing.

Christel R. Devadawson, a Cambridge-Nehru scholar from

Girton for her PhD, is Professor, Department of English, University of Delhi, where she supervises research in contemporary South Asian life-writing, detective fiction, and popular visual culture. Devadawson is currently working on a manuscript on the visual politics of Lockwood Kipling. Her most recent publication in the field of Visual Studies is 'Visuality, spectacle and "the common good" in India today' (University of Roehampton, 2017). She curated the exhibition entitled *Legacies of Laughter, Legacies of Loss: Pictorial Satire in Postindependent India* for *Samanvaya,* the Indian Literature Festival, 2015. Devadawson's books include *Out of Line: Cartoons, Caricature and Contemporary India* (Orient Blackswan, Delhi, 2014), and *Reading India, Writing England* (Macmillan, Delhi, 2005).

She has served as Head, Department of English, University of Delhi (2015-18) and Head, Department of English, at St. Stephen's College, University of Delhi.

Jonathan Gil Harris is Professor of English at Ashoka University, where he has also served as Founding Dean. He is best known to Indian readers as author of the best-selling *The First Firangis* (Aleph Book Company, 2015). Prior to moving to India in 2013, Harris was Professor of English at George Washington University. A scholar of Shakespeare, he served as associate editor of *Shakespeare Quarterly* from 2005 to 2013, and was also president of the Shakespeare Society of India from 2014 to 2018. He is the author of many books on Shakespeare and early modern culture, including *Foreign Bodies and the Body Politic* (Cambridge University Press, 1998), *Sick Economies: Drama, Mercantilism and Disease in Shakespeare's England* (University Penn Press, 2004), *Untimely Matter in the Time of Shakespeare* (University Penn Press, 2009), *Shakespeare and Literary Theory* (Oxford University Press, 2011), *Marvellous Repossessions: The Tempest and the Waking Dream of Paradise* (Ronsdale, 2012), and, most recently, *Masala Shakespeare: How a Firangi Writer Became Indian* (Aleph Book Company, 2018).

Hemachandran Karah teaches English Literature at the Humanities and Social Sciences faculty, IIT Madras. He is interested in researching on themes such as disability, health, language question, literary criticism, and musicology. The hallmark of humanities scholarship lies in its rare capacity to enrich responsible worldviews, empathy, justice, and care. Karah's activism as a teacher and a scholar caters to such a goal. In addition to academic writing, Karah regularly contributes to newspapers and magazines.

Raj Kumar is Professor and Head in the Department of English, University of Delhi. His research areas include autobiographical studies, Dalit literature, Indian writing in English, Odia literature and postcolonial studies. He has been a Fellow at the Indian Institute of Advanced Study, Shimla in 1999 and has published in journals such as *Social Action, Sateertha Bulletin, The Fourth World, Creative Forum, Language Forum, Jadavpur Journal of Comparative Literature, Indian Literature, Social Scientist, Journal of the School of Language, Literature and Culture Studies, International Journal of Communication, Rama Devi Women's University Journal of Social Sciences and Humanities, International Journal of Religious Tourism and Pilgrimage, Ravenshaw Journal of Literary and Cultural Studies, Economic and Political Weekly,* and *Studies in Humanities and Social Sciences.* Raj Kumar has also translated literary texts from Indian languages, especially Odia into English. His book, *Dalit Personal Narratives: Reading Caste, Nation and Identity* has been published by Orient BlackSwan, New Delhi in 2010 and reprinted in 2011, 2015 and 2017. His English translation of Akhila Naik's *Bheda*, the first Odia Dalit novel is published by Oxford University Press, Delhi in 2017. His book *Dalit Literature and Criticism* is published by Orient BlackSwan, New Delhi in 2019.

Rama Mathew is an ELT consultant and retired as Professor of Education from the University of Delhi in 2016 where she was also Dean of the Faculty of Education. She taught at the EFL

University (Hyderabad) for several years. She has directed many ELT projects in India. She was Head of the Research, Monitoring and Evaluation Unit of *English in Action* project in Bangladesh in 2015 and later served as a Consultant. She has been involved in several teacher development and assessment projects, and published articles and books in the area. Teacher education, in particular working with teachers on Continuing Professional Development (CPD) projects, has given her the motivation and sustenance to keep growing and developing.

Recently she worked (with Annamaria Pinter from the University of Warwick, UK) on a project titled *Children and Teachers as Co-researchers in Indian Primary Classrooms*. She was the lead coordinator of AARMS (2018-19), an Action Research Mentor Scheme (2018-19) and now the lead mentor of ELTRMS (English Language Teaching Research Mentoring Scheme), both British Council initiatives. Her research interests include language assessment, teaching English to young learners, Continuing Professional Development of teachers, and making English accessible to learners online. She is currently the President of AINET (All India Network of English Teachers), a community of people interested in the teaching and learning of English in India.

Makarand R. Paranjape is currently Director, Indian Institute of Advanced Study, Shimla. He was educated at St. Stephen's College, Delhi, and the University of Illinois at Urbana-Champaign, where he earned a Masters and PhD in English. He has been Professor of English at Jawaharlal Nehru University for eighteen of his thirty-eight years as university teacher. He is the author of some twenty and editor of over two-dozen books, in addition to hundreds of academic papers and popular articles. His latest books include *Debating the 'Post' Condition in India* (Routledge, 2018), *Cultural Politics in Modern India* (Routledge, 2016), and *The Death and Afterlife of Mahatma Gandhi* (Penguin Random House, 2015). Makarand is currently a columnist in *DNA, Mail Today*, and *The Print*.

N.S. Prabhu has a Masters degree in English Literature from Madras University and a Masters as well as a Doctoral degree in Linguistic Science from the University of Reading. He taught English in undergraduate colleges for about ten years, and then did a year's Diploma in Teaching English at the Central Institute of English, Hyderabad. He went on to work at the British Council in Madras for the next twenty years, giving advice and short courses on teaching English at undergraduate colleges in southern India, before going on to teach Applied Linguistics at National University of Singapore for ten years. His best-known publications are *English Through Reading* (Macmillan Education, 1974) and *Second Language Pedagogy* (Oxford University Press, 1987).

G.J.V. Prasad is Professor of English at Jawaharlal Nehru University, India and former Director of the Jawaharlal Nehru Institute of Advanced Study, JNU. His major research interests are Indian English Literature, Contemporary Theatre, Dalit Writings, Australian Literature, and Translation Theory. He has co-edited with Sara Rai a collection of stories from Indian languages, *Imaging the Other*. His academic publications include *Writing India, Writing English: Literature, Language. Location* (Routledge, 2011) and *Continuities in Indian English Poetry: Nation, Language, Form* (Pencraft International, 1999). His edited volumes include *Translation and Culture: Indian Perspectives, Vikram Seth: An Anthology of Recent Criticism* and *The Lost Temper: Essays on Look Back in Anger*. His co-edited collections include *Disability in Translation: The Indian Experience* (with Someshwar Sati), *'Violets in a Crucible': Translating the Orient* (with Madhu Benoit and Susan Blattes), *Indian English and Vernacular India* (with Makarand R. Paranjape). His forthcoming publications include a monograph on Khushwant Singh and an edited volume on translation. Prasad is also a poet and a novelist, and has most notably received the Katha award for translation from Tamil.

Pete Sharma works as a lecturer in EAP (English for Academic Purposes) at Warwick University, UK. He is a Director of Pete Sharma Associates Ltd, a consultancy and training organization (www.psa.eu.com). Pete worked for many years in Business English as a teacher trainer and materials writer. He is a regular presenter at conferences around the world, giving plenary talks, keynote speeches and workshops. Pete is the co-author of several books on technology including *Blended Learning* (2007), *400 Ideas for Interactive Whiteboards* (2011) in the Macmillan 'Books for Teachers' series and most recently, *Best Practices for Blended Learning* (2018). His e-books are on 'apps' in Business English (2013) and how to write for digital media (2014). He has contributed the chapter on 'Evaluating Digital Materials' in the *Routledge Handbook of Materials Development for Language Teachers* and 'Virtual Reality in English Language Teaching' for *Digital Innovations in Language Teaching* (Learning Technology SIG), both forthcoming. Pete was the Newsletter Editor of the IATEFL (International Association of English Language Teachers) CALL (Computer-assisted language teaching) *Review* (2008-09) and has a Masters in Educational Technology and English Language Teaching from Manchester University. Pete loves travel and yoga and has enjoyed personal and professional visits to India.

Shobha Sinha has a PhD (Elementary Education) from the University of Illinois at Urbana-Champaign, USA. She is an Associate Professor in the Department of Education, University of Delhi. She teaches courses in language and literacy. Her research interests include early literacy, literacy in the classroom context and literacy development of children from marginalized background and low literacy homes.

Pushpinder Syal, PhD from Lancaster University UK, is Professor, Department of English and Cultural Studies, Panjab University Chandigarh where she has been teaching since 1978. She was also Director at the Lucknow Campus of the

English and Foreign Language University in 2010-11. She has worked and guided extensive research in the field of stylistics, language teaching and literature and has several publications in these areas, chiefly *Structure and Style in Commonwealth Literature* (Vikas, 1994), *An Introduction to Linguistics: Language, Grammar and Semantics* (Prentice Hall, 1997) and was guest editor of *Language and Language Teaching-13,* and contributor to journals of language and linguistics. She is a recipient of Commonwealth Academic Staff Scholarship, Charles Wallace Fellowship and Australia India Council Award, and has presented papers in national and international conferences. In literature, she has taught and researched in African, Australian and Indian writing. She has been associated with several projects with the British Council, CBSC, NCERT, IGNOU, etc. being deeply involved in teacher education and evaluation, and her current interests have expanded to translation, Sikh Studies and literature in Punjabi. She lives in Chandigarh and does organic farming and voluntary service for animals.

Jackie-Lynn Van Tilburgh has an MA and TEFL certification from Wright State University, Dayton, Ohio. She worked in India in 2015 as part of the English Language Fellow Program that sends TESOL educators around the globe to work with students, teachers, and teacher educators to improve English instruction and promote better cross-cultural understanding. Prior to that she had been an Instructor in Bridging and IEP (Ohio Northern University), and English Program Instructor (Wright State University).

Harish Trivedi, formerly Professor and Head of the Department of English, University of Delhi, studied English and Sanskrit at the University of Allahabad and has a PhD from Britain on Virginia Woolf. He taught briefly at the University of Allahabad and the BHU (1967-69), and then at St. Stephen's College, Delhi (1969-84) and the University of Delhi (1984-2012). He was a Visiting Professor at the University of Chicago (1999,

2011) and the University of London (2002-03). He has authored *Colonial Transactions: English Literature and India* (Calcutta 1993; Manchester 1995), and co-edited *Interdisciplinary Alter-natives in Comparative Literature* (New Delhi 2013), *The Nation across the World: Postcolonial Literary Representations* (New Delhi and New York 2007), *Literature and Nation: Britain and India 1800-1990* (London 2000), *Post-Colonial Translation: Theory and Practice* (London 1999), and *Interrogating Post-Colonialism: Theory, Text and Context* (Shimla 1996; rpt. 2000, 2006), etc. He has also translated Premchand's biography by Amrit Rai, *Premchand: His Life and Times* (New Delhi 1982, rpt. 1991) and writes in both Hindi and English. Currently, he is one of the contributing editors of an international project based in Stockholm for writing a history of World Literature.

Penny Ur was educated at the Universities of Oxford (MA), Cambridge (PGCE) and Reading (MATEFL). She emigrated to Israel in 1967. She has thirty years' experience as an English teacher in primary and secondary schools in Israel. Now retired, she has taught courses at BA and MA level at Oranim Academic College of Education and Haifa University, and has lectured extensively in language teachers' conferences worldwide. She is interested in all aspects of language-teaching methodology, but in particular issues of vocabulary and grammar in language teaching, and language-learning activity design. She has published extensively, and was for ten years the editor of the Cambridge Handbooks for Language Teachers series. Her books include *Five Minute Activities* (co-authored with Andrew Wright, 1992), *Grammar Practice Activities* (2nd edition, 2009), *Vocabulary Activities* (2012), *A Course in English Language Teaching* (2012), and *Discussions and More* (forthcoming) all published by Cambridge University Press.

Editors and Interviewers

Editors

Rachna Sethi is Assistant Professor in the Department of English, Rajdhani College, University of Delhi. She won the Katha Award for translation from Hindi in 2004. She has been an Associate at the Indian Institute of Advanced Study (IIAS), Shimla. Her areas of interest are postcolonial literature, urban studies, gender studies and language teaching. She has published extensively in both national and international journals on areas of urban studies and gender studies. She is currently the President of FORTELL and has had a long association with it in various capacities. Apart from academics, she is enthusiastic about travel and photography.

A.L. Khanna retired as Associate Professor from Department of English, Rajdhani College, University of Delhi. His interests include Applied Linguistics, materials production, evaluation and assessment. He is currently engaged in ELT materials development and teacher training projects. He has published extensively in prestigious journals. He has several ELT books for young learners to his credit. He has also been closely associated with the NCERT and several SCERTs across the country. He co-edits with R.K. Agnihotri the Sage series on *Applied Linguistics*. He is one of the Chief Editors of *Language and Language Teaching*, and the Coordinating Editor of *FORTELL*.

Interviewers

Tara Chadha retired as Associate Professor of English from Shyama Prasad Mukherji College, University of Delhi. She has been associated with SCERT, NCERT, IGNOU, NIOS, and several other bodies in the field of English Language Teaching. She is currently teaching at Netaji Subhas University of Technology as a guest faculty. She was also associated with GGISPU and the British Council as a teacher.

Tara has been conducting Teacher Training workshops for reputed publishers like Pearson, Headwords, etc. for over two decades. She has also written more than half a dozen books for SCERT, NIOS, Pearson and University of Delhi.

Manjari Chaturvedi teaches English literature and language at Motilal Nehru College, University of Delhi. She is a PhD candidate at the Jawaharlal Nehru University, Delhi, working on multi-generic representations of Nana Saheb, a key leader in the 1857 rebellion in India. She has been a Fulbright visitor (Foreign Language Teaching Assistant) in 2016-17 at Florida International University, Miami, USA in the Department of Modern Languages where she taught Hindi language. Her interest areas include Cultural Studies, Post-colonial Studies, Language Teaching, and Film Studies.

Gitanjali Chawla is an Associate Professor of English at Maharaja Agrasen College, University of Delhi. She is a folklorist, researcher, editor and materials producer; her research on the folk songs of Punjab has led to an active participation in several fora, both at the national and international level and has several publications in journals of repute to her credit. She has also dabbled in translation and is keenly interested in innovative pedagogies in the virtual mode. She is the co-editor of three seminal anthologies, *Cultures of the Indigenous: India and Beyond* (2014), *De-territorialising Diversities: Literatures of the Indigenous and Marginalised* (2014) and *Re-storying the Indigenous and the Popular Imaginary* (2017). She has also been the Presidential International Visiting Scholar 2018, Wheelock College, Boston University, Boston, USA.

Iqbal Judge retired as Professor from the Department of English, Post Graduate Government College for Girls, Chandigarh. With a specialization in ELT, she has taught for about 36 years at the undergraduate and postgraduate level in Punjab and Chandigarh. Her core interests are in materials production and classroom teaching, particularly using bilingual materials with students from disadvantaged backgrounds. Over the years, she has presented numerous papers at conferences, published articles and books, written course materials for IGNOU and conducted workshops for teachers and students. Having retired in 2018, she now devotes her time to running gender sensitization and menstrual and adolescent health awareness sessions in schools, as changemaker with change.org.

Prachi Kalra teaches in the Department of Elementary Education at Gargi College, University of Delhi. She teaches courses in the pedagogy of language and literacy. Her main areas of interest are children's literature and storytelling. She has recently completed her PhD on how stories can enable a critical pedagogy in the elementary classroom.

Ruchi Kaushik is Associate Professor of English at Shri Ram College of Commerce, University of Delhi. She specializes in materials production and teacher training in ELT. Her research is on designing needs-based learning materials for business students and she has been actively involved in curriculum development and materials production projects at Delhi University, IGNOU and NCERT. In 2013, she co-authored the book *Language, Literature and Creativity* (Orient Blackswan) and in 2014 *Listening and Speaking XI* (Cambridge University Press). She was awarded the US State Department Award to present a paper at the 50th TESOL 2016 International English Language Convention held at Maryland, USA. She was also one of the Delhi University delegates invited for an intensive training in Blended Learning Methodology held at the Open

University, Milton Keynes, UK. She is currently the Vice-President of FORTELL.

Barun Kumar Mishra is Assistant Professor of English at Rajdhani College, University of Delhi. He has been actively involved in research of English language teaching in India. He has published two articles in the Hindi journal *Kal ke Liye* on socio-cultural aspects of the Hindi belt. Mishra has translated *Problematising English in India* for Eklavya Prakashan, funded by Ratan Tata Foundation and also authored e-lessons on 'Translation and Interpreting' for ILLL, University of Delhi. He has to his credit a book on Rabindranath Tagore. He is a certified trainer of English to the working professionals of the Aviation Industry.

Aarati Mujumdar is the Head, Department of General Education, Modern College of Business and Science, Muscat, Oman. She taught at M.S. University Baroda for 26 years and joined MCBS in 2014, where she now teaches Academic Writing, Business Writing, Technical Writing and World Literature. She holds a PhD and an MPhil degree in ELT from M.S. University, Baroda, India. Both dissertations are psycholinguistic, exploring the cognitive processes of writing L2 compositions.

She has researched and published extensively in areas of developing Critical Thinking, Teaching Methodologies, and Classroom Research. She has co-authored books on Business Communication and English for Academic Purposes. Her recent book *Teaching English as Second Language: Theory and Praxis* is used as a textbook and a reference book.

Lina Mukhopadhyay is an Associate Professor in the School of English Language Education, the English and Foreign Languages University, Hyderabad, India. Her research interests are Second Language Acquisition, Reading Development, Language Assessment and Testing, and Bi/multilingual

Education and she has publications in each of these areas. She is currently involved in a multilingual education project in collaboration with the University of Cambridge and funded by the ESRC-DFID, UK. The five-year long project is examining the interrelatedness of language of instruction, school skills, and cognition of young learners studying in challenging contexts in government low aid primary schools in India.

Sabina Pillai teaches at Shaheed Bhagat Singh (Evening) College, University of Delhi. A former civil servant, she is an alumna of Lady Shri Ram College and JNU. She has published research papers and presented at national and international conferences. She was awarded the annual Cambridge Teacher Training Award at IATEFL 2014 in the UK. Her book *Spoken English for My World* (2016), published by Oxford University Press has been translated into Hindi. She has co-authored *Soft Skills and Employability Skills* (2018), published by Cambridge University Press. She is a leading resource person for teacher development workshops in the country.

Nupur Samuel teaches English language proficiency and teacher education courses at Ambedkar University, Delhi, India. She is interested in English language assessment, critical thinking, writing pedagogy and teacher education, and developing teaching-learning materials and tests. Nupur's doctoral work on Dynamic Assessment of writing focused on examining if assessment and teaching could be seen as unified activities, aimed at assisting students develop their writing abilities while they were in the process of being assessed. Nupur is an alumna of the International Visitor Leadership Program (2013) of the US Department of State's premier professional exchange programme and has presented papers at various national and international conferences.

Mukti Sanyal is Officiating Principal in Bharati College, University of Delhi. Over the last 35 years, she has been active in spearheading dialogue on issues related to pedagogy and language teaching, making it possible for many national and international experts reach college and school teachers in Delhi.

She was awarded the Best Lecturer for Bharati College for the year 2016-17. She was awarded a grant to attend the 41st Annual TESOL Convention in Seattle, WA in 2007. She is part of the external faculty of the English and Foreign Languages University (EFLU), Hyderabad.

She has co-authored course books that are part of syllabi in the University of Delhi and other universities. Titles like *Fluency in English I & II* and *English at the Workplace I & II* were well received. She has been a resource person and materials writer for the University of Delhi, NCERT, NIOS, SCERT, DIETs (District Institute of Educational Training), Oxford University Press and Macmillan.

Tasneem Shahnaaz is Associate Professor in the Department of English, Sri Aurobindo College, University of Delhi. She is interested in English language teaching, South Asian studies, translation, feminist and cultural studies. She has published reviews and literary articles in scholarly journals and critical anthologies. She writes poetry which has been published in many poetry journals in India and abroad. She has co-authored a Delhi University textbook, *Business English* (Pearson, 2008), for BCom students, *English and Communication Skills* Parts I & II (Cambridge University Press, 2015 and 2016) for polytechnic students. Her other publications include *Translation: Principles and Practice* (Primus Books, 2017) and *Crossing Borders* (Fairleigh Dickinson University Press, USA, 2017).

Chandra Nisha Singh retired as Associate Professor from Lakshmibai College, University of Delhi. She has researched extensively in the area of Gender Studies, and has focused on women writers in Hindi and English. Her book, *Radical Feminism and Women's Writing: Only So Far and No Further*

(2007) deals with various facets of gender studies. She also got deeply involved with the disabled community when she joined the Equal Opportunity Cell of the University of Delhi as its first OSD and worked for their rights, resources and social acceptance. She is currently working on the biography of J.L. Kaul, a blind social activist who is venerated for his selfless activism.

Mona Sinha is Associate Professor in the Department of English, Maharaja Agrasen College, University of Delhi, where she has been teaching literature, language, development and cultural studies for more than two decades. She is currently a researcher in the area of television and gender studies. Her varied publications include translations, papers on feminist studies, media and culture, besides articles on language proficiency. Her long years of teaching have led to an active interest in the evolving needs of the students with respect to pedagogy and methodologies for the teaching/learning of language and literature.

Prem Kumari Srivastava, a recipient of several postdoctoral fellowships and awards, with three decades of research and teaching experience at IIT Delhi and University of Delhi, is Associate Professor of English at Maharaja Agrasen College, University of Delhi. Some of her seminal works are *Leslie Fiedler: Critic, Provocateur, Pop Culture Guru* (2014), McFarland & Inc. Publishers, North Carolina, USA; three volume series (co-edited) on *Literatures, Languages and Cultures of the Indigenous,* in 2014 and 2017 published by Authorspress Publishers, Delhi and *Revisiting American Literature* (co-edited) Macmillan Publishers India Pvt. Ltd (2018). Her association with FORTELL and the *FORTELL* Journal goes back a long way. Her research displays an overarching focus on gender, the popular and the indigenous; American Literature and Innovative English Language Materials Production.